ATHLETIC IDENTITY

INVINCIBLE AND INVISIBLE
THE PERSONAL DEVELOPMENT OF
THE ATHLETE

D1617087

First Edition Design Publishing

Athletic Identity: Invincible and Invisible,
the Personal Development of the Athlete
Copyright ©2015 Personal Player Development, LLC

ISBN 978-1622-877-44-7 PRINT
ISBN 978-1622-877-45-4 EBOOK

LCCN 2014954790

January 2015

Published and Distributed by
First Edition Design Publishing, Inc.
P.O. Box 20217, Sarasota, FL 34276-3217
www.firsteditiondesignpublishing.com

I dedicate this book to Lindsay and our three boys Nathan, Marcus and Rhys as well as my family and all the individuals who enter and exit the world of sports and competition.

I want to thank the athletes and helping professionals for their contributions to the contents of this book, Dr. Elizabeth Rockstroh for her assistance and Johnny Duggan for believing in the Athletic Identity movement.

This book is in loving memory of my father Mark D Robinson Jr., my friend Mr. Bill Cook and my uncle, James (Gus) Waller, rest easy.

Athletic Identity

Invincible and Invisible
The Personal Development of the Athlete

Dr. Mark Robinson, Ph.D.

TABLE OF CONTENTS

ATHLETIC IDENTITY: INVINCIBLE AND INVISIBLE, THE PERSONAL DEVELOPMENT OF THE ATHLETE

Chapter One
Memoir of an Athlete

I have fought the good fight, I have finished the race, I have kept the faith [2 Timothy 4:7]

Introduction

We are each guided towards different careers and passions by our life experiences. My journey, through participation in sports, ultimately led me to work in the area of personal development of athletes. My life story will help you understand my intention for the creation of this book.

Middle and High School

I first started playing basketball with my Uncle Gus when I was about twelve years old. Uncle Gus always watched basketball and enjoyed playing on the weekends at Balboa Park in Reseda, California. He would take me to the park with him, and I would sit and watch the games. When there were not enough players for five-on-five games, he would let me play. I think this was when I first fell in love with basketball.

Mark Robinson experiencing youth basketball

I did not have the opportunity to attend any developmental youth camps as a child, but I did play one year in a youth league called the

Chatsworth Chiefs while in middle school. As a youth my parental and living situation played a significant role in my emotional state during the K-12 section of my journey. I was angry at the world because of my distant relationship with my father, which led me to behave in a way that was academically destructive and at times criminal.

This negative behavior caused me to attend two junior high schools in Southern California, Northridge and Nobel Junior High School. I originally attended Northridge but transferred to Nobel. I transferred because I became involved in several fights on the way to and from school as a result of the racial lines dividing the neighborhood. I also attended three high schools in Southern California from 1983 to 1985: Cleveland, Chatsworth and Simi Valley. Cleveland High School was walking distance to my house, had a great basketball reputation, and I had friends who attended there. I received the opportunity to play junior varsity (JV) basketball my first year. After playing JV, I was determined to make the varsity team. As a result, I stole a set of keys from the custodian's office and used the keys to gain access to the gym at night, so that I could shoot around. All I wanted to do was get better. Unfortunately, as a result of stealing the keys, I was expelled. This was a difficult time for me; I thought the JV coach, an African American man named Bobby Braswell, would come to my aid and defend me, but he never showed his face or spoke on my behalf during the entire process of my expulsion. His lack of support left me with a negative opinion of basketball coaches, specifically African American coaches, and I was no longer interested in playing basketball.

My expulsion from Cleveland then led me to attend Chatsworth High School. My time at Chatsworth lasted less than a year because I used a knife to defend myself against three other students. They had attempted to jump me after an altercation I had with another student. The boys did not attend the school. Too my recollection, they were much older than I was at the time. Regardless of the circumstance, this stunt resulted in an arrest. Too afraid to call my mother, I called my Uncle Gus who came to the police station and took me home. As a result of my actions, my mother demanded that I leave home and move in with my father, who lived in Simi Valley.

However, transferring to Simi Valley High School was a turning point because of the students at Simi Valley. This was the first time I was in an educational environment that was dominated by white youth. With the exception of my cousin and three other black boys on the track team, the rest of the students were white. Up until this point I had attended institutions with large numbers of African Americans and Latinos. Unlike the horror stories regarding African Americans feeling isolated on a predominately white campus, I was welcomed and was consistently encouraged to do my best academically.

The head coach was a Caucasian man named Bob Hawking. He was a great motivator and asked me if I wanted to play on the basketball team. He explained that the team had just graduated a few key players, most notably Marty Wilson, who received a basketball scholarship to attend Pepperdine University. He continued to clarify that the team could use an athlete like me. Initially I had reservations, but my mom convinced me that I would benefit from playing on the team. I played my senior year and truly enjoyed the experience. The guys on the team and coaching staff were encouraging, and like the other students at Simi Valley, they took a real interest in my academic development. The team captain, Christian Aurand, would ask how I was doing in class or if I needed any help on a daily basis. Coach Bob Hawking was a man of integrity and discipline and was constantly concerned about my well-being. I cannot recall a day without him asking me "What can I do for you?" or "Do you need anything?" He would often tell me that he wished he would have had me as a student for all four years of high school.

My senior year was non-stop. Since I was now attending my third high school, my academic transcript was filled with D's and F's. The Simi Valley High School counselors informed me that academically I was far behind the requirements needed to graduate. In order for me to graduate on time, I would have to attend night school for the entire year to make up the lost credits. I managed to graduate on time with a 2.01 GPA, but I lacked the necessary core courses to attend a traditional four-year institution. My only option was to attend a community college.

COMMUNITY COLLEGE

In 1985, Jim Harrick was the head basketball coach at Pepperdine University and had expressed interest in me during my senior year of high school. I was excited about the possibility of attending Pepperdine because I had been to a few of their games to watch Marty Wilson play. Pepperdine is located in Malibu California, has a beautiful campus overlooking the Pacific Ocean and was a place I enjoyed visiting. After learning about my academic situation, Coach Harrick suggested I attend City College of San Francisco (CCSF). If all went well after two years at CCSF he would offer me a scholarship to attend Pepperdine. Brad Duggan, a strong Irish Caucasian, was the men's basketball coach at CCSF at that time, and he contacted me to determine if I was interested. He said "I am Brad Duggan, and I coach at CCSF. If you want to win and become a better basketball player, then come and play for me. If you don't, that's fine but remember this: when we play against you, we will beat you." With that argument, I ended up attending CCSF and played for Coach Duggan. While playing for him, I developed a great relationship with Coach Duggan; a relationship I cherish to this day. Although he was a tough coach, he had a genuine interest in the development of all his players. Coach Duggan, like Coach Hawking, was concerned about my well-being and would always tell me that "there is an invisible sign above my door, and it says, 'No Unsolicited Advice,' so if you have a problem or an issue you need to bring it to me." Coach Duggan would tell us to give 100% in practice and games, to stay out of trouble (but if trouble found you he had your back, at least the first time), and to enjoy San Francisco. I liked the last piece of advice the most.

During my two years at CCSF I grew as a person and had a wonderful time playing with a great group of guys including: Dean Garrett, Joe Asberry, Troy Berry, Edward Topper Allen, Steve Johnson, and Steve Macintosh. The team took two trips to China as part of a sister city exchange project, which opened my eyes to the world at large. Basketball was going better than ever for me, and I did improve as Coach Duggan promised, and we did win. Off the court, Coach Duggan landed me a job working for Burns International as a security guard. I was assigned to work the 50-yard line for the San Francisco 49er games and at a bus station located in downtown San Francisco in the Tenderloin district.

From left to right, Mark Robinson, Chris Walker and Kevin Stafford. CCSF basketball trip to China 1986

As a result of my success in basketball at the community college level I now realize, that's when my identity started to change and I entered the world of athletic identity. I started receiving interest from colleges across the country and wondered to myself, "why now?" I asked myself, "Why didn't any of these colleges contact me when I was in high school?" My heart was set on Pepperdine because the campus was close to home. I spent a lot of time there while attending Simi Valley High School, and I knew Marty Wilson really enjoyed playing at Pepperdine. However, Coach Duggan insisted that I take a few visits to make sure Pepperdine was the place for me. I visited Tulsa, Indiana University (IU), and Pepperdine in that order. Dean Garett, a former CCSF teammate, received a basketball scholarship to IU the year prior to my graduation and told me how great IU was for him. I did have a wonderful time on my visit to IU, but my goal was to become a Pepperdine Wave.

While at Pepperdine, Coach Harrick asked who was recruiting me and how many visits I had taken. After I told him I had visited Indiana and met with Bob Knight, he explained that playing for Bob Knight would be an opportunity of a lifetime and suggested I take that scholarship. I was disappointed and at the same time touched by his sincere approach towards what he thought was best for me. My academic performance while at CCSF was not stellar, but I managed to graduate with an associate's degree and had again achieved a 2.01 GPA. The Associate of Arts degree and my GPA were good enough to transfer to the next level. I accepted the scholarship to attend IU, and the following year Coach Harrick left Pepperdine and accepted the head coaching position at the University of California in Los Angeles. Maybe this was a coincidence, or maybe coach Harrick knew he was leaving Pepperdine, but either way his encouragement for me to attend IU was genuine.

THE BLOOMINGTON INDIANA EXPERIENCE

When I arrived in Bloomington during the summer of 1987, the men's basketball team had just won the national championship. The town was buzzing about the game-winning shot that Keith Smart made to win against Syracuse. The returning players included: Ricky Calloway, Keith Smart, Joe Hillman, and Brian Sloan. They were nothing like I expected, and neither were the incoming high school players, particularly Jay Edwards and Lyndon Jones. Back then, Edwards and Jones were known as " Co Mr. Basketball" in the state of Indiana. I had assumed that I would run into a few cocky, arrogant guys who would brag about being National Champions.   Jay and Lyndon won three straight high school championships, and I had also expected them to boast. However, none of that ever happened. The most humble group of champions I have ever been associated with were my teammates at IU.

Indiana University Basketball Team, 1987-1988 Season. Mark Robinson #10

Indiana University Basketball, 1988-1989 Season

Playing for Bob Knight at Indiana elevated one's status in the community and on campus, and no one loved the recognition more than myself. This was the first time I truly felt entitled as a result of the hard work and commitment I made at the high school and community college level. Now this might sound silly, but the fact that people recognized me and wanted my autograph, fed into my ego. The social life of an Indiana basketball player could take one of two courses. You could a: take the student athlete route and focus on academics and basketball, or b: take the rock star route while focusing on academics and basketball. Most of my teammates took route A. I, however, took route B. Yes, the rock star route. I think my decision was due to my ignorance regarding what IU basketball was all about. I did not grow up in basketball culture like most of my teammates, and I suspect they knew what signing up for IU basketball entailed. I had no clue.

Taking the rock star route had serious consequences because Coach Knight and his staff knew everything players did after practice and games. Some students would even call the basketball office and leave messages for coaches alerting them that some of the basketball players were out at a party. My social life affected my playing time. Although the consequences frustrated me at times, I still made my choice. Once I was able to accept the coach's decision, it did not matter how much I played during games. I believed my personal time existed before or after the games, and I loved each and every minute of that lifestyle. My job was to give 100% on the basketball court in practice and in games, and I did that without question. However, I felt once basketball was over, my time was available to do as I pleased. If IU granted a degree in the area of being a socialite, I would have not only made the honor roll, but I would have been the valedictorian of my class.

As part of a nationally recognized athletic program, athletes are afforded certain luxuries, and one extravagance was having team managers around. Many on the outside do not realize the difficulty involved with being a team manager nor do they see the long-term benefits. Lawrence Frank, who would later become an NBA coach, and I established a great relationship. He was a guy who would tell you how he felt in a joking, yet sarcastic way and did not care about who you were and how many minutes you were playing. I enjoyed laughing and talking to "L," as we called him, because he could put a tough practice or loss in a humorous perspective even when you did not want to laugh. He would also give you a certain look at times to alert you that Coach Knight was not in the mood for playing around and that locker room jokes needed to be shut down.

My relationship with Coach Knight was not like the relationship I had with my previous two coaches to say the least. Coach Knight would often ask me to just leave and go back to California. Although I gave that option some thought, I enjoyed being in the Rock Star mode way too much and going back to California was not an option. During my tenure, players like Rick Calloway, Dave Minor, Chuck White, and Lawrence Funderburke transferred for a variety of reasons. At the time, I could not understand why a player in his right mind would leave Bloomington. I developed a relationship with all of these guys and each time one of them transferred, I was hurt in the same way a person feels the loss of a family member.

Coach Knight, while misunderstood by many on the outside world, treated all players, starters, and reserves the same. His methods of motivation were nothing like I had ever seen. He placed a big emphasis on diversity and would often go into a rage if he walked into a pre-game meal and the room was segregated. No table with black-only players was allowed, and vise versa. Additionally, there were two issues that were not debatable with Coach Knight: alcohol and drugs and academics. Players would simply no longer be at IU if they had trouble in either of these two areas.

As time passed, players would often speak to me about personal issues they were having; for some reason I was the type of athlete who had the ability to make players feel comfortable when speaking to me. In return, I would listen because I found the issues fascinating. Although at the time I was not qualified to give an expert opinion, I accepted my role on the team and on a social level, which might have allowed players to open up to me about how they were feeling.

As players transferred from the team, my compassion for them and my curiosity in athletic behavior began to grow. The one thing I noticed when these athletes left IU was the amount of isolation the institution quickly, yet unknowingly placed them in. Once a player made the decision to leave IU, they were on their own and kept a distance between themselves and former teammates. None of the players' departure hurt me more than when Jay Edwards left IU and entered the NBA draft after his sophomore season. Jay Edwards had the best jump shot and highest basketball IQ of any player I had ever worked with, but when he decided to turn professional, I questioned the rationale for his decision. He and I spent two years together regularly, and we never discussed the possibility of him playing in the NBA. I believe playing in the NBA was one of his long-term goals, but leaving after his sophomore year was the result of his family's expectation. Once the decision was made, the IU basketball community turned on Jay and he was placed in isolation.

My rock star attitude took a toll on the IU assistant coaches at the time. Dan Dakich and Joby Wright both challenged me with intense verbal confrontations on separate occasions. Ron Felling simply ignored me most of the time unless I humored his jokes. Tates Locke, on the other hand, was the one coach who was able to relate to me. One day Coach Locke and I sat high in the stands in Assembly Hall, and he asked me why I was attending IU? I think he expected me to say something along the lines of "to become a professional basketball player" or "to earn a degree." My reply was one in which I stood by: "to experience all that college has to offer." Coach Locke laughed, and as the conversation continued, he gave me much needed insight on how college coaching is designed and how the system was affecting my playing time as well as basketball players just like me all over the country.

Coach Locke quickly began to explain his view of coaching at the division 1 level. He said that every student athlete has an advocate on staff trying to get their player minutes on the court. They do this because in most cases they recruited that player. When a player does not perform to expectations on and off the court, the head coach usually blames the assistant coach who was responsible for the recruitment process. When that assistant coach gives up on the athlete, dealing with that player becomes the responsibility of another assistant coach. The process continues until the team runs out of assistant coaches. Then a decision is made to either encourage the player to leave or to let the athlete ride the scholarship out. When I said I understood, he said, "I am the last assistant coach on the list to deal with Mark Robinson." Whether this was true or he was just trying to get me to leave the rock star mode, based off the behavior of the other assistant coaches, his reasoning made complete sense. We left Assembly Hall, and I felt much better about my interactions with Coach Wright and Coach Dakich. I understood that these assistant coaches were under extreme pressure, and it is sometimes easy to forget that the players dealt with are 18-21 year old kids. I also came to understand that as a player, once practice was over I could go back to my rock star world, and they had to continue to stay in the world of Bob Knight.

While at IU, Buzz Kurpius was the team's academic advisor, and she did a wonderful job of keeping the team eligible. I majored in General Studies, but I had no clue what I could do with a degree in General Studies and neither did anyone else. Buzz was a sincere person, and most of the time it was clear that she wanted the best for the guys on the team. Her job was to make sure players attended class and passed classes. However, her oversight did not extend beyond our class work. At the time, everyone assumed athletes were gaining the necessary personal development and becoming better people through the basketball experience. Understanding the personal needs of the athletes on the basketball team was not a high priority, and the importance of personal development was unknown. I would argue that many athletic advisors today are still unaware of the needs and benefits of personal development for athletes.

During the spring semester of 1988 my GPA did not meet the standard that Coach Knight believed to be acceptable. As a punishment, he assigned me to work during that summer at a company called Cook Group Incorporated. I did not know much about the company or what I would be doing, but since the work assigned was a punishment, I assumed it would not be pleasant. I reported to work and sat with Mr. Bill Cook, the CEO. I remember seeing Mr. Cook around Assembly Hall from time to time and had exchanged pleasantries with him and his wife, Gayle, on several occasions without ever realizing he was the CEO of a major company. On my first day we talked and laughed for a little over an hour while watching his marching band on tape. While I was enjoying this opportunity, Mr. Cook received a call from Coach Knight asking what job I would be doing? Mr. Cook replied to Coach that we had not yet begun that discussion. Coach Knight asked Mr. Cook to give me the dirtiest job he could find. I ended up cleaning bathrooms, maintaining a bird pool in front of the office, and sand blasting vents on the roof of the building all summer. However, every time Mr. Cook and I got an opportunity to chat, we would. After the summer job, I did not see much of Mr. Cook until I finished my degree.

As an athlete you can quickly become the target of judgment because of the expectations supporters, coaches and fans place on you. Being a target is something athletes including myself had difficulty embracing. In the fall semester of 1988, I had the pleasure of meeting Bob Miller who was the Monroe County prosecutor at the time. Although the reason why our paths crossed was not ideal, I believe he saved my life by simply looking at the facts of the criminal cases presented to his office. Another IU player and I unknowingly found ourselves in hot water, and although we were scared and nervous while the investigators reviewed the case, the evidence clearly showed that we had done absolutely nothing wrong. However, when dealing with the justice system, being black in the state of Indiana means that sometimes right and wrong do not matter. Luckily for us, this was one of those occasions where justice did prevail. After the ordeal was concluded and put to rest, Bob Miller told me that if I ever wanted a job in the prosecutor's office to give him a call. I did not know what I could do in that office, but I told him that I was grateful for the offer.

ATHLETIC IDENTITY: INVINCIBLE AND INVISIBLE,
THE PERSONAL DEVELOPMENT OF THE ATHLETE

In May of 1990 I graduated with a degree in General Studies and yet again had a GPA of 2.01. Like most athletes, graduation was a difficult time for me. I spent the next two years trying to figure my life out. At times, I felt isolated from the world I had become accustomed to enjoying. I had no idea what to do or who to call. My scholarship was gone, and I had no money. I had heard about the Continental Basketball Association (CBA) tryout for the Quad-City Thunder and attended in hopes of landing a spot on the team. The coach made it clear that he was only selecting two players from the tryout to attend training camp. I do not know how, but I was one of the two selected out of the fifty trying out.

I spent a few months with the team and played enough minutes in each game to satisfy myself. During that time I had five different roommates, and it was strange to me that a team could just bring a guy in for a few days and then cut him. Seeing what these guys went through as they unpacked, just to pack up again days later, was something I could not get used to. I never really got to know any of them except a guy named Robert Mukes. Rob, as he liked to be called, had experience playing overseas and was a veteran player. Rob schooled me in the business of how professional sports worked from the athletes' perspective on both the domestic and international level. He told me the best thing for me would be to play overseas because I would have a better experience and earn more money. He would often say "if these players did not play basketball they would have a hard time adjusting to the real world, because basketball is all they know."

After our conversations about the comings and goings of players, I knew the best thing for me was to try and land a job overseas. According to Rob, the closer the NBA trade deadline, the more likely we would see changes. He made it clear that we were not immune to these changes. As the NBA's trade deadline approached, veteran players became nervous and argumentative about playing time and shots. I was cut at the NBA deadline and I found myself actually feeling exactly what several players felt who were cut from the team in the previous months. This was the first time in my life I had been cut from a team. I had a feeling of devastation combined with an intoxication of self-doubt. I headed back to Bloomington to figure out my next move. As I traveled back to Bloomington, Indiana, I seriously considered moving back to California to live near my family. The shame of not making it in semi-pro basketball, and the feeling of not having a career direction all spun around in my head.

Back in Bloomington, I remembered Bob Miller, the Monroe County prosecutor, who told me if I ever wanted a job to give him a call. I did call him and was hired to work in the pre-trial diversion program for the Monroe County Prosecutor's Office. This was a program dealing with first time offenders who wanted to avoid trial. These individuals were mainly students who were cited for public intoxication. Instead of an overseas professional basketball job, I had a 9-5 office job. I was not pleased working normal hours, but the work helped me survive.

My supervisor at the time was Linda Bough. Linda was easy going, polite, and would often speak to me about graduate school and the implications for my future. She often suggested I look into sports psychology or counseling athletes. In her opinion, they need a special type of counseling. She thought I would be good at this type of work because we often talked about the problems associated with being an athlete. She encouraged me to take one day off from work and visit some of the graduate schools on the Indiana University campus to see if I was interested—so I did. While on the IU campus, I ran into Steve Downing, a former IU player and longtime IU Associate Athletic Director. He suggested I speak to Coach Knight as I went through this transition. From a player's perspective, Steve had a solid relationship with Coach Knight, and from the outside they seemed close. Trusting his advice, I made an appointment to see Coach.

One of the first things Coach Knight asked me was, "What do you want to do?" I enjoyed college life and the life of an athlete so much that I never really thought about my next move in detail. In my mind, I was still holding on to the college athlete experience. I finally answered him by saying graduate school or basketball overseas. He replied firmly that he thought I should attend graduate school. Coach Knight explained that I could always play overseas after graduate school and even offered to call whoever I wanted him to so that I could play, but not until I finished graduate school.

During this same time I was alerted that Mr. Cook had a Bloomington based adult travel Amateur Athletic Union (AAU) team loaded with former IU players and a few other college basketball players from the state of Indiana. Somehow I was offered a place on the team and began to travel around the Midwest playing in tournaments between 1990 and 1994. The travel, accommodations, and being associated with really great guys on a team was just like being back in college. Many of the guys on the team worked for the company, were in some line of business with the company, or were trying like hell to get involved with the company. I guess you could say long before enterprise started hiring athletes; Mr. Cook was leading the way. Guys like Chuck Franz, Scott May, Mike

Woodson, Joe Hillman, Wayne Raford, Eddie Bird (yes, the brother of Larry) and Indiana State's Carl Nicks, were involved with the team.

My Mom and I happy times while on break from IU.

As I spent more time playing with the team and my relationship with Mr. Cook grew, he asked me the same question Coach Knight asked me only months prior, "What do you want to do?" By then I made up my mind to attend graduate school. I expressed to him that I would be attending graduate school and then playing overseas, but I needed to find a job that would fit in my class schedule. At that time, many university graduate programs did not cater to working adults. He offered me a factory position with Cook Group Incorporated, but I expressed to him that I wanted to find something on campus. A week or so later Chuck Franz called and told me that Mr. Cook wanted me to know if I attended IU graduate school, that financially, I would have no worries and he would seek out a scholarship to take care of whatever I needed. I took the opportunity of attending graduate school in order to allow me to fully understand what made athletes tick. I enrolled in the School of Education's Counseling and Guidance program and focused on the mental health track.

During my athletic career at IU I developed great relationships with a number of people in the Bloomington community. I was now entering graduate school and wondered what types of relationships I would build as a former student athlete. I admit the transition was difficult but once I was able to connect with insightful, like-minded people while going through this transition it became easier.   Between 1992 and1994, my roommate in graduate school was a guy named Ozie (O) Davis. O was a former Miami University of Ohio football player who was attending IU law school. O loved basketball and consistently reminded me about what a great opportunity athletes had. We would sit up sometimes all night and talk about athlete behavior. O was a socialite on the black frat scene. Since I was a former athlete from the socialite scene, we put our heads together and threw regular social events at the Bloomington Elks Lodge, located on the edge of Bloomington.

After having to sneak around to campus parties as an athlete myself, I wanted to offer events athletes could attend without the worry of getting in trouble with the athletic department or Coach Knight for having what we called "the student experience." Additionally, I wanted to make sure none of the athletes who attended our events would end up with a driving under the influence or a date rape charge. We also had a number of cookouts at our apartment where we would invite a select number of people, athletes included, for the purpose of educating them from a personal development perspective. This social side of graduate school gave me an opportunity to research athlete behavior as well as help athletes deal with being a student athlete on the IU campus. Up until this point, I never really understood what it meant to be humble. However, as a former athlete now attending graduate school, athletes from all sports gave me a high level of respect. Athletes consistently told me that they were proud of me for making the move to graduate school. O repeatedly pushed me to stay focused on athlete behavior in my graduate program as he knew this was an area that needed attention. We would often discuss athlete behavior and what institutions should do to help athletes develop personally.

One of the benefits of going through the transition from athlete to former athlete was the control over time. As an athlete the sport and other people dictate your time for so long, I rarely had the chance to slow down and take in the entire experience. I was now in a position to control my time and more importantly I was able to understand and appreciate those around me. During this time I began to fully understand the amount of wealth Mr. Cook possessed. He was by all accounts the wealthiest man in the state of Indiana. During my last year of graduate school, Mr. Cook told me he was thinking about buying an international basketball team. He first wanted to send our AAU team to the United Kingdom to play against some of the teams. He wanted to see if his decision was a wise investment. I was part of the team selected, and we had a blast. I was offered a few jobs while on the trip but had to decline, since I needed to finish graduate school.

In graduate school I flourished academically, probably because this was the first time I studied something of interest to me, athlete behavior. Although the course work did not focus on athletes, I made sure my approach towards the relevant theories, research papers, and assignments always focused on the athlete, his behavior, and counseling methods. I learned that the most notable theorists in counseling failed to include the athlete in any of their sample population. These pioneers include Freud, Jung, and Skinner. Also, most of the research conducted involving athlete behavior was incorrect based on my personal experiences as well as my observations of other athletes. This was particularly true of research about athletes feeling inferior on predominately white campuses. I often wondered who found any credibility in the existing research, and I wanted to know which black athletes were included in these studies.

I finished the program in 1994 with a 3.8 GPA, which at the time pleasantly surprised me. After graduation Coach Knight called me into his office and congratulated me on obtaining my master's degree. During our conversation, I finally asked him a question that haunted me for years. I asked, "Coach, why do players transfer and leave IU?" He answered simply, "Mark, that is a simple question. They leave because they do not get the recognition they think they deserve from me."

At the time, I did not realize how influential my time playing for Coach Knight would be. Years later, I understood that the recognition Coach Knight gave his players was not on the court while they were playing, It is the public recognition we all receive for the rest of our lives from the experience of playing for him at Indiana University.

Each year, I call Coach Knight to wish him a happy birthday, as do nearly all of his former players. We do this to show our respect to him, and our gratitude for the experience he gave us, as well as the recognition we all now receive. As mentioned previously, my relationship with Coach Knight was not like my former relationships with other coaches, but due to our specific relationship, I have been able to flourish.

All the experiences that transpired while I was an athlete in Simi Valley, San Francisco and Indiana, from academic adjustments, social relationships, getting into trouble to working as a security guard, to working for Mr. Cook, were all elements of personal player development, as I will describe in this book. Only through these experiences, and by playing for Bob Hawking, Brad Duggan and Coach Knight, was I able to have the opportunity to play basketball and study on an international level. I will always be eternally grateful for the opportunity to play for Bob Hawking, Brad Duggan and Coach Knight.

INTERNATIONAL

Once my final year of graduate school was complete, the word was out that Mr. Cook did indeed purchase a team in Manchester, England. The team was called the Manchester Giants, and the coach at the time, Mike Hanks, would be hosting tryouts in Bloomington. I attended the tryouts and made the team, but I had one serious problem. I now had my sights set on enrolling in a doctoral program in order to gain a deeper understanding of athlete behavior and to develop a method to assist in their personal development.

I expressed my reservations to Mr. Cook, and he laughed. He then told me that there were schools in the United Kingdom, and that all I needed to do was pick one and apply; the finances would also be taken care of with the same scholarship used for my master's program. I applied to a few schools and was accepted into the Victorian University of Manchester in the fall of 1994. Mr. Cook, a very kind and generous man, made it clear that my association with the team had nothing to do with the scholarship towards my education. He let me know that if I was cut from the team, he would continue to make sure that everything was taken care of in order for me to finish my Ph.D.

I signed a contract to play for the Manchester Giants and although my overall experience in Bloomington was tremendously enjoyable, it did not compare to my time in the UK. My goal as a kid was never to play basketball on TV, have my face on trains and in advertisements, or to have my own radio show. However, that is what ended up happening when I started to play for the Giants. The city, the people, and my teammates were all wonderful, and the environment was a perfect fit for my rock star attitude and way of life. While the basketball area of my life was going well, my academics were again flourishing.

The research for my doctoral program originally had a focus on black athlete behavior, but once I started to collect data, I opened my research to all athletes. I did not exclude anyone from the data collection process because I learned quickly that athletic behavior encompasses all races. I traveled the globe interviewing professional athletes about their collegiate experience and investigated the personal development components needed by athletes to be successful. Belgium, France, Switzerland, Germany, Ireland, Austria, the Netherlands, Central America, and the United States were all places I interviewed athletes. Originally, I thought interviewing athletes on the subject would be challenging.

However, once participants learned I was a former player of Bob Knight, I could not get them to stop talking. One of the many things I learned about athletes during this time was that we all had personal issues we were either currently dealing with or had dealt with that was clearly associated with sports participation. Additionally, the services we required were not available while we attended college and were not offered at the professional international or post collegiate level.

Manchester Giants Basketball, Manchester England

While playing and studying in the UK, I witnessed players being cut from their teams in England,. This bothered me because I remember the feeling when I was released from the CBA. Many of these players knew I had my master's degree and was studying for my Ph.D., and assumed I was a good resource to seek out. After getting cut from teams, players would call me and ask for my advice. I learned that their contracts were not being honored, and that opportunities for personal development were not being afforded to players. Of more significance was that the players' only option was to find another team because basketball was all they knew. The league and teams had no formal introduction for players, no educational pathway for young English players, and very low salaries for the English players. Yet perhaps the most serious issue I encountered was the emotional toll that being cut from a team took on players.

Mr. Cook would often visit Manchester to see how the team and organization was developing. On one of Mr. Cook's visits to the UK, we talked about the problems in UK basketball, and he suggested that I get involved with the players union in the UK or start one myself. Soon after his visit, I contacted English players that I knew would be interested in establishing a players union. I talked with England internationals like Carl Brown, Yorick Williams, Steve Bucknell, and Colin Irish. I also called on veteran American players like John Trezvant, Ted Barry, and Tony Dorsey. We held elections, and I was appointed CEO of the Basketball Players Association UK. Within one month we signed up 120 players in a league that had 130 players. I quickly began to send out newsletters about the state of the league and suggested players contact me regarding issues they were having. Many players that contacted me were more interested in getting help with personal development issues than with basketball issues. At this time, I had been involved in helping players across the league. My master's degree in counseling gave me the necessary confidence to work with athletes on a variety of personal development issues.

Manchester Giants basketball, Manchester England

After a few years playing for the Manchester Giants, it was determined that a coaching change was needed. I received a call from an African American professional named Jim Brandon, the Sheffield Sharks coach—the team was located about 40 miles east of Manchester. Jim wanted the

Manchester job really bad, and so did most coaches in England. Mr. Cook owned the team, and they all knew he was committed to basketball. Jim called me every day for two weeks leading up to his interview, and I gave him the necessary information I thought he needed to land the job. I told other coaches that called me the same thing. After a few weeks, they announced that the Giants had hired Jim Brandon. I knew I had another year on my contract as well as one year to finish my dissertation, so I was looking forward to working with Jim. I was soon called to a meeting with Jim Brandon and Scott May in the lobby of the Crown Plaza Hotel in downtown Manchester. Scott May, a former IU basketball great, business partner and close friend of Mr. Cook [and the first African American legitimate business man I ever met], oversaw the managing of the Giants at that time. After brief pleasantries, Jim told me he was not going to bring me back to the team next year. He stated that he wanted to move in a different direction; he wanted the team to be the focus and not Mark Robinson. I wanted to leap across the table and strangle him, not because he was cutting me, but because he used me for information about the team to get the job and lied to me regarding my role on the team along the way. This was the first time I learned that professional sports is a take-no-prisoners business.

Nevertheless, I called Scott later and discussed my options moving forward. I still had a year left in my doctorate program and unless I signed with a local team, arrangements had to be made for me to stay in England and finish my degree. Finding a team interested in me was difficult because as a player I was hot tempered and demanded excellence from players and coaches; clearly I was a Bob Knight product. Some teams wanted my talents, but they did not want my attitude. Also the owners did not agree with the idea of a players union. I ended up signing a contract with the Sheffield Sharks and focused on finishing my Ph.D. After signing with Sheffield, I desperately wanted to win a cup final or championship, which I was not able to do in Manchester. I was very agitated at the critics—they reported that I was a good player, an all-star player but could not win a cup final.

The Sheffield Sharks hired Chris Finch as their coach, a former player for the Sharks [who later became the coach for Great Britain and in the NBA] who was not highly skilled as a player but played hard and knew how to win. Although this was Coach Finch's first year coaching I felt he had a high level understanding of the game of basketball and the team could be successful, so I was excited to play for him. Soon after we started playing I realized we needed more size if were going to be able to make a run for one of the championships in British basketball. I heard about a 6'9" English international player who had just been released from a club in Europe named John Amaechi. I saw John at one of our games in London and asked if he had any interest in playing with us, and he said he was interested. The team and John began negotiating his contract. There was a rumor that John was gay, and that was the reason he was released from his previous team. Players asked me about this while others attempted to inform me that John might be gay. The contract negotiation took a while. Although the deal eventually was completed, the process did not happen without question and concern. As a teammate, John was and is a true professional and a strong advocate for the development and treatment of English players. We often discussed the problems associated with both British and American basketball, players' behavior and mentality. John was never a fan of Americans playing in England. After spending time with John, it was clear to me that he was gay. Although that was his business, I knew that at some point I would have to answer the question because my association with him continued to grow. As predicted, I began receiving questions about John's sexuality from players throughout the league. My answer was simple: "If he is gay, what business is it of yours?" The questions coming to me died quickly as players began to see my friendship with John grow. Years later, John did announce publicly that he in fact was gay. This did not surprise me. My time in Sheffield ended on a high note both academically and athletically. We won a cup final the very same week I successfully defended my doctoral work.

Sheffield Sharks Cup Final Champions, 1998

ATHLETIC IDENTITY: INVINCIBLE AND INVISIBLE,
THE PERSONAL DEVELOPMENT OF THE ATHLETE

Lindsay and I after the doctorate graduation, 1998

The English process of defending a doctorate is much different from the United States version. Your dissertation is sent to five to seven professors from other universities in the UK, and no one on the committee is from your institution. I guess this is a process to make sure internal politics stay out of the way. My doctoral oral defense took 35 minutes, and the committee commended me on making a significant contribution to knowledge. I was excited and charged to break into the field of personal development for athletes; at that time this was called life skills at the college level. Once I completed my doctorate, my interest in basketball quickly began to fade. I did however, play on several different teams before deciding to try and put my education to use. I was now helping players beyond England. I began receiving calls from Germany, France, and Italy from players requesting help in the area of personal development. All of the players came from some of America's top university athletic programs which led me to the conclusion that these players were not being afforded the necessary personal development from their respected institutions.

The Asian Experience, Hong Kong

Birmingham Bullets basketball, Birmingham England

HIGHER EDUCATION AS A PROFESSIONAL

I returned to the San Francisco Bay Area in 2000 and set up a series of meetings with community college administrators in hopes of landing a job in counseling or athletics. Most of the community colleges had a lengthy hiring process. Unless you were already a part-time employee, you had little chance of being hired. My network was very small since I had been out of the country for many years studying and playing basketball. .

I contacted Coach Knight and asked him to call David Stern in hopes of getting a job working with the player development division in the NBA, and he did. Mr. Stern allegedly reviewed my resume and kindly sent me a "if anything comes up that fits your skill set, we will let you know" email. Upon return to San Francisco, I also contacted a number of division one colleges and offered to present a series of workshops for their athletes based on my research. Every college I contacted regarding my research told me that their athletes were great, and the athletic department had certain programs in place that already covered personal development. Although I was confident that this was not the case for many athletic departments, I continued my quest to assist athletes and the athletic community on a larger scale. The facts were that no one knew me; I had no credibility in the United States, and I was not in the "good 'ole boy" network. This meant that visiting campuses was not going to happen. I quickly realized that regardless of my athletic background, academic experience, and practical work in personal development for athletes, working with athletes in the United States was a long shot.

Throughout this career-hunting process I visited with my former coach, Brad Duggan, who was now the Department Chair of the Physical Education and Dance department at City College of San Francisco (CCSF). Brad and I discussed old times. After about twenty minutes into the conversation, he turned the topic to my future and asked what I wanted to do. I explained what my research was on and how I worked with athletes in the area of personal development for years. Brad suggested that I meet the CCSF basketball coach Harry Panazopilious. Harry was a great guy who had a huge heart when it came to the student athletes on his team. The man would literately give kids the last dollar in his pocket to make sure they had something to eat. We got along instantly, and Harry asked if I could work with his players regarding the off-the-court stuff. I was very excited to get this opportunity. I would be able to use the work from my master's and doctoral research. More importantly, I would be able to work with athletes in a setting where I believed the findings from my research would be the most effective.

I was hired as an academic counselor for CCSF in the New Student Counseling Department, but my assignment was in the Athletic Department. The college was able to offer positions under what is called an emergency hire. This basically means that a person has a specific skill set that few people have, and the need to bring that person on board is an emergency. These positions are part-time, but if the hire is successful then a full-time position is possible.

I quickly proved to be a worthy hire; all of the student athletes I worked with graduated and transferred to four-year institutions. Although my job description was heavily weighted with academic planning, I spent most of my time working with athletes in the area of personal development. The academic planning process was easy for me as you only have a certain number of classes an athlete can take in a given semester because of the time allocated for athletics. Based on an athlete's placement test scores in English and Math, you then have to find the classes in which athletes can be academically successful. The planning process is that simple.

After a few years of working part-time, I was hired full-time and granted early tenure at CCSF as an academic faculty member. Soon after the promotion came the opportunity to move into an administrative position. Between 2005 and 2010, I held positions as Associate Dean, Dean, and ultimately became the Vice Chancellor for Student Development. During this administrative climb, I continued to work with athletes who either contacted me or who were referred to me by friends and associates. I was still trying to get an opportunity to visit four-year campuses and deliver workshops for athletes on the topic of personal development. I reached out to my alma mater, the IU athletic department, but they would not consider having me on campus because I was part of the Coach Knight legacy. I called Mike Davis in 2001 and, I called Kelvin Samson in 2006. Both African American coaches would not return any of my calls.

As a community college administrator, I was afforded the luxury of receiving the best professional development opportunities available. Although I had the necessary degrees, I felt I needed to be trained to be an effective administrator. I was accepted into the Harvard Institute for Educational Management (IEM), and the American Council for Education (ACE) Fellows Program in 2008 [ACE is the major coordinating body for all of the nation's higher education institutions]. Both programs gave me the needed growth to become a community college president. These elite programs also fostered my creativity and gave me the necessary push to change my direction from becoming a community college president to fulfilling my goal to become a personal player development consultant.

One of the requirements of the yearlong ACE fellowship program was for participants to choose any college in the country where they felt they could conduct research and learn from being on that campus. I selected Pepperdine University, and they approved having me on campus. I was excited to finally get the opportunity to be associated with Pepperdine after so many years. The president of Pepperdine at the time was Andy Benton, who is a man of God but also a straight shooter in regards to running the institution. His number one priority was to make sure the students attending Pepperdine had the necessary resources to become successful. His close second was to continue to find efforts to diversify the student body, faculty and staff. Without question, the force driving his priorities was raising money for the institution. He and his staff welcomed me with open arms, particularly Marnie Duke Mitze his Associate Vice President and Chief of Staff.

President Benton allowed me to travel to several countries to conduct research on the possibilities of athletes participating in international programs outside of their respected sport seasons. Pepperdine has campuses in Switzerland, Germany, England, and Italy. Once again, I had the opportunity to examine athletes from a global perspective and also engage with athletes from a variety of sports. The research allowed me to use my experience in the personal development of athletes to assist many individuals I came in contact with while traveling abroad.

A really exciting component of my ACE fellowship was my weeklong visit at the National Collegiate Athletic Association (NCAA) headquarters in Indianapolis, Indiana, to review their CHAMPS/Life skills program as well as interview the president of the NCAA at that time, Myles Brand. My interview with Dr. Brand was done to gather information regarding the NCAA's position on personal development of athletes. Dr. Brand and I never met before this opportunity; however, he was previously the president at IU, and the man that many say was behind the firing of my former coach, Bob Knight. Our meeting lasted about an hour and a half. During the meeting, Dr. Brand gave me his ideology for what a holistic personal development program should consist of for NCAA student athletes.

I found his position on the personal development of athletes both genuine and full of concern for student athletes. However, at several points during our conversation he clarified that these were his opinions and not the view of the NCAA. Some of his opinions included identifying that most NCAA member institutions think they have personal development programs in place even though they do not. Additionally, he noted that member institutions are concerned with winning, eligibility, and graduation because that is what they are judged on. He further noted that it would be beneficial to focus on personal development of the athlete. However, the question would then become how to assess growth, and who is and who is not providing development opportunities correctly. Dr. Brand explained that the question of funding for personal development programs for many institutions would be an issue, and that the implementation would therefore be challenging. At the same time, he recognized that these programs are greatly needed and there is real value in personal development off the field. Finally, Dr. Brand discussed the NCAA's CHAMPS/Life Skills program but admitted that no substantial research existed to prove this approach was correct. He noted that the program may work for some student athletes but may not work well for others.

Once my yearlong ACE fellowship was complete, I returned to CCSF to assume my administrative duties. During my absence there was a change in leadership, and the chancellor who originally hired me was no longer with the institution. More importantly, I realized that I had changed and no longer had the drive to become a community college president. My new supervisor, Chancellor Don Griffin, had a number of issues with the way I wanted to move forward in creating programs. At that time, I had deans reporting to me who were making six figure salaries and were virtually doing nothing to earn their paychecks.

I pushed my subordinates to be more creative and develop better programs and also to put the interest of the students above their paychecks. This was considered by many to be "rocking the boat." It did not take long for one of the deans to file a complaint against me. At the time I did not realize that my boss was waiting for this. He placed me on administrative leave pending the outcome of the investigation. In the end, the conclusion proved I did nothing wrong.

The administration I would have gone back to work with did not understand the athletic mentality nor had they ever been athletes. With this realization, I understood that my return to an administrative position at CCSF would not work because I was not willing to change. As athletes, we are used to competition as well as daily, weekly, monthly, and seasonal goals. The community college landscape does not share this mindset. Instead, community colleges survive by accepting money from the state year after year without any true accountability for the success of the students on their campuses. Community colleges are not judged on the number of students they graduate or transfer; they judge themselves on the number of programs they offer regardless of the lack of success these programs may have. Conducting research in the community college setting in order to address problems for student athletes, is not encouraged.

Spending a year at Pepperdine changed me in a significant, positive way. The Pepperdine campus has a small chapel overlooking the Pacific

Ocean, and I began to explore my Christian faith. I visited the chapel daily, and this simple routine was one of the things I missed most upon my return to the Bay Area. The fellowship experience reminded me of my original intent while obtaining my master's and doctoral degrees, running the Basketball Players Association in the UK, and accepting my academic faculty position at CCSF. During these times I had a specific focus on helping athletes become better people. I understood that although their journey through sport participation was individually unique, there were common struggles among athletes. I now realize that over the years I allowed the difficulty of working with NCAA member institutions in the area of personal development, and the lure of the community college administrative salary, to derail my original intent.

BACK ON TRACK

Two years after my ACE fellowship, I resigned from administration. I returned to my tenured academic counseling position with an intentional goal of building my personal development practice for athletes. With this renewed focus, I took some time to review the landscape of personal development for athletes in our current society. I called Keith Smart, a former IU teammate and NBA coach, and began to inquire about the programs and services the NBA offered while explaining to him what my goals were. Keith told me that what I was talking about was on a different level than what NBA teams offer, and although they have employees in the position of player development, the knowledge and experience I had on the subject was advanced. I then placed a call to Lawrence Frank, the former IU manager and NBA coach, and asked him some of the same questions I posed to Keith. Lawrence told me that the need for what I was doing was significant at the NBA level, but that teams were simply not providing services and resources to the magnitude I was suggesting. These two conversations energized me and catapulted my previous assumptions and research findings on the personal development of the athlete.

When I first started researching personal development and athlete behavior in 1995, the Internet and social media were virtually nonexistent. Most people in the workforce were using the intranet, an internal way of communicating for company employees. However, over the years technology advanced. As a result, disseminating and gathering information has become much easier. Social media has also made it much easier to witness the personal development problems and needs athletes encounter daily. More importantly, with advancement in technology and communication, organizations can no longer hide their weaknesses in the area of personal development for athletes.

As I searched the Internet and again researched athlete behavior, I learned that many of the issues that I researched were not being addressed. For years, coaches, athletic directors, advisors, and the like were able to hide the huge need for the personal development of the athlete. I had been told repeatedly for many years that student athletes and professional athlete organizations were on top of the personal development issues of their athletes. Many institutions also alerted me to the fact that they had African American coaches and staff members who provided assistance in dealing with their athletes' personal development. This was far from the truth based on my experience with African American coaches. The new reality is that these institutions and organizations were able to conceal their lack luster approach to providing holistic programs for athletes because there was not a vehicle, such as social media, to report on the issues and problems associated with athletic behavior which is directly related to personal development.

After concluding market research, I knew the world of athletics did not have access to information solely dedicated to the personal development of athletes nor was the subject of athletic identity presented in a beneficial way for the athlete. However, from my previous experience with the athletic community, I knew I had to find people in the network of athletics to interview on subjects that struck to the core of personal development of athletes. I interviewed people who were considered industry experts and individuals who have worked with athletes in athletic departments across the country on the subject of personal development of athletes. Most importantly, I interviewed athletes who provided their opinion on a variety of areas I have researched for years.

I already had a plethora of my own content, to deliver on the subject of personal development for athletes. The combination of my own content, and the collection of interviews I conducted, gave me the fuel to make what I call my first public significant contribution to knowledge in the field of personal development for athletes.

In 2013 I launched Personal Player Development Magazine: www.ppdmag.com. I used social media to attract viewership as well as give critics and naysayers the opportunity to challenge the need and authenticity of not only my work, but the overall subject matter of personal development of athletes. The magazine quickly became known as a significant resource for all involved in the athletic environment. The feedback from members of the athletic community on all levels validated the need for more attention towards the personal development of athletes, the lack of overall understanding of athlete behavior, and a significant need to understand athletic identity, and the role identity plays within the developmental process of our athletes.

This book is my second contribution to knowledge in the field of personal development for athletes. The subsequent chapters include research findings combined with years of experience working with athletes on personal development issues in a practical environment, as well as the opinions and valid facts from members of the athletic community at all levels of sport. The subject of this book, athletic identity, is a journey all athletes experience and the personal development during this experience is the missing link. Both athletic identity and personal development have been the cornerstone of my practical application when working with athletes. I hope you enjoy the journey.

Dr. Mark D Robinson
Make Life Your Sport

Chapter Two
Personal Development

We are hard pressed on every side, but not crushed; perplexed, but not in despair; persecuted, but not abandoned; struck down, but not destroyed [2 Corinthians 4:8-10]

Introducing Personal Player Development

Each year, millions of people worldwide attend personal development conferences and workshops. Two types of people attend these events. The first are individuals looking to better themselves, and the second are people seeking to become a life coach. While the need to become a better person is important, you have to wonder what happened to these people in college. Why didn't they receive the necessary education and guidance to become successful during four years of college? The answer is as simple as it is disappointing; most colleges do not focus on personal development for students. This is why so many college graduates end up leaving their selected careers and venturing into the life coach arena.

Personal Development courses first began appearing in the early 1970's in California. Their popularity quickly gained them a reputation for weekend quick fixes that were quirky and off the wall.[1] By the 1980's, organizations running personal development courses had sprung up around the world. The first decade of the new millennia was witness to the industry morphing into various areas of specialization, such as courses in assertiveness, business success, and trauma counseling. Seen from an outsider's perspective, this was the period during which the industry turned professional.

Personal development includes activities that improve awareness and identity, develop talents and potential, build human capital and facilitate employability, enhance quality of life, and contribute to the realization of dreams and aspirations. Personal development is a field of practice and research. As a field of research, personal development topics increasingly appear in scientific journals, higher education reviews, management journals, and business books.[2]

While respecting the history, definition, and field of research, we still must ask: How does personal development connect to the athlete in theory and practice? More importantly, we must ask how researchers study subjects and implement findings to assist athletes in the area of personal development since this population was never the specific intended audience. Unfortunately in sports, personal development programs have become a "check-the-box and move-on" concept.

A Brief History of Personal Development for Athletes

The history of Personal Development for athletes has its origins in two sectors, the college sector, and the professional sector. Both areas recognized the need to develop programs that focused on the personal development of athletes in order to help these players become better people. Although the sectors identified the need for personal development, an actual understanding of the key elements required to develop a holistic approach for programs has only recently become a major priority.

Community and Junior Colleges

The National Junior College Athletic Association (NJCAA) is the only national governing body of intercollegiate athletics for two-year colleges. The NJCAA has a current membership of 520 institutions, which is second only to its counterpart at the four-year level, the National Collegiate Athletic Association (NCAA).

The NJCAA had a program called Leaders for Life, which they tried to encourage member colleges to utilize. This program consisted of a course developed by a former officer within the NJCAA and focused on decision making, developing leadership skills, and planning for the future. Unfortunately, this program did not resonate with member colleges. Mary Ellen Leicht, Executive Director of the NJCAA, reported that, "When we surveyed our colleges as to why, we were told many colleges already had similar college-wide, non-sport specific programs in place."3 As a result, the NJCAA discontinued the use of that program, but they continue to encourage colleges to provide life skills training to student athletes.

National Association of Intercollegiate Athletics

According to the National Association of Intercollegiate Athletics (NAIA) President Jim Carr, the focus on personal development for the NAIA started about a decade ago. Carr states the rationale behind personal development was, "we really wanted to put some more structures in place and formalize what the coaches and administrators have been doing on their own for about 75 years in NAIA schools, and that is build people of character through athletics and higher education."4

Currently, the NAIA offers a program called Champions For Character. This is a character program offering training for coaches, combined with a recently implemented online program for student athletes. The focus of the program is centered around "trying to make sure that our student athletes and coaches are behaving on the court, on the field in a way that is consistent with champions of character."[5] Further, there is a focus on conduct and competition, a scorecard that measures how schools are doing in a number of different areas, as well as outreach into the community.

NATIONAL COLLEGIATE ATHLETIC ASSOCIATION

The mission of the National Collegiate Athletic Association (NCAA) is to maintain intercollegiate athletics as an integral part of the campus educational program, and the student athlete as an integral part of the student body. With this in mind, the CHAMPS/Life Skills program was created to support the student athlete development initiatives of NCAA member institutions, and to enhance the quality of the student athlete experience within the context of higher education.

According to the NCAA, in 1991, the NCAA Foundation initiated efforts to create a total development program for student athletes. Through the collaborative efforts of the NCAA Foundation and the Division 1A Athletics Directors' Association, the *CHAMPS/Life Skills* program (Challenging Athletes' Minds for Personal Success) was created.

In 1994, after several years of development by the NCAA Foundation, the *CHAMPS/Life Skills* program was introduced to the NCAA membership. That summer, 46 NCAA institutions participated in the first orientation for administrators from around the country. Since then, approximately 40 member institutions and conferences have joined the *CHAMPS/Life Skills* program each year.

Participants in the *CHAMPS/Life Skills* program were provided with instructional materials and supplemental resources that supported a student athlete's development in five areas: academics, athletics, personal development, career development, and community service. The specific problem and challenge in the five areas is centered on the topic of personal development.

Academics, career development, athletics, and community service are the topic areas institutions focus on. However, the area of personal development has been overlooked and many think that the four outlined areas consist of a personal development program. Personal development is its own topic encompassing these four areas. What the NCAA and member institutions have done, and continue to do, is provide an illusion that the four areas are the backbone of personal development.

As a component of development, NCAA institutions are invited to nominate student athletes to attend the annual NCAA National Student Athlete Development Conference held each spring. The mission of the conference is to assemble a diverse group of student athletes who will actively participate in and experience a multitude of challenging and thought-provoking activities. This will enable them to become change agents on their campuses and in their communities. The problem with this annual event is that most of the invited student athletes are handpicked by the athletic department and are usually student athletes coming from the top tier of the academic and socioeconomic background ladder. The athletes who truly need personal development are rarely invited to this event.

Today, the NCAA education services staff oversees the development of the program, offering services, support, and programs to participating institutions throughout the year. The *CHAMPS/Life Skills* program is supported through the promotional and financial efforts of the NCAA. However, implementing this program was too difficult for the NCAA to manage, and the organization turned the responsibility over to individual institutions. Therefore the question must be asked: Who is monitoring the personal development programs for student athletes at NCAA member institutions? Further: How is curriculum and true training for helping professionals being implemented?

The NAIA and the NCAA programs both lack the substance needed in the area of personal development as defined later in this book. A comprehensive approach to personal development is based on understanding the curriculum topics student athletes require when viewed from a holistic development perspective.

Professional Sector NFL

The professional sector, particularly the National Football League (NFL), has been the most dedicated and aggressive in their appreciation of personal development programs for athletes.

In 1991, the NFL developed player programs, but the concept did not have the attraction from players and the teams. In 1992, the idea was reintroduced again. Dr. Lem Burnham was the director at the time, and then John Woten and his staff started the movement in 1992. Bill Walsh, the great 49er head coach, developed programming for the 49ers players that dealt with life issues faced by the athletes. It was not until 1993-94 that player development programs were rolled out in terms of brochures and tapes combined with a marketing piece.[6]

Lamonte Winston, one of the first full-time player development employees with an NFL team, described his experience and the history of player development programs in an interview:

> The formality of player engagement was originally called Player Programs; it was just a brochure. So with player programs I can say there were just four main components: there was continuing education, internship opportunities, family assistance, and financial education. At first, teams had anybody in the club they could appoint to fill this role.
>
> I spent seventeen years at the Kansas City Chiefs (KCC) and literately jumped into it, and we began to just do things as an organization. The philosophy was just around our players in the KCC organization. Lamar Hunt, who was our owner and founder of the Chiefs, is a visionary. He was very, very supportive of player programs. Over the years, we began to develop and grow and players became involved in internships. We had guys going back to school. We dealt with family issues, [and we] started giving education, real life education, through the players' lives.
>
> I suggested we take our rookies and have a series of seminars and we had our own rookie seminars at KCC. There came a point where obviously people in the NFL recognized what we were doing in Kansas City; the other teams recognized it. The NFL league office took the concept.
>
> The NFL league office then introduced the rookie symposium, and so that was kind of the birth if you will. The NFL league office adopted what we did in KCC so today it is the rookie symposium, which I think is fantastic. It's a fantastic experience, the transition piece for players that are drafted. The one thing that it didn't address was the needs of the un-drafted rookies that make your team. The KCC provided a rookie symposium for our un-drafted rookies.
>
> Then the league mandated that every club had to be represented in the player programs area. Every team had to have a club coordinator at the time, and I saw that

move from just being the grounds crew guy or the ticket guy or the lady that works in marketing to some people who were really kind of qualified to really work with players. Then we moved from player programs, [and] it morphed in my mind into development; Player Program was the official name.

But really when you're working with players and you're starting to teach, you're starting to change behavior, and it really becomes development. The KCC just rebranded our programs and we just started calling it Player Development, and I changed my title to go along with that. A year or two later, the NFL as a whole got the concept, and they rebranded Player Programs into Player Development.

Since that time, the concept of the Player Development division has grown by leaps and bounds in the NFL. The Player Development division in the NFL has gone through some leadership changes; Mike Cain was our vice president for a number of years and currently it's Troy Vincent. Troy was a former player in the NFL for 18 years, and he had his thoughts about what it should be and how players would be more up to being involved and engaged in the program. He wanted that word engagement to really mean that players have to engage in the things that we develop in terms of giving them resources to help them grow. Therefore, Troy rebranded player development to Player Engagement.[7]

PAADS

The Professional Association of Athlete Development Specialists (PAADS) is probably the oldest independent professional organization working in the field of personal development for athletes. The organization was created from an Annual Athlete Development Summit, a concept originally created by the National Football League Players Association (NFLPA) and hosted by the NFL in 2002. In conjunction with the NBA, the Athlete Development Summit was expanded in 2003 to include additional leagues and athlete development experts. Since then, the Athlete Development Summit has continued to provide a forum for the exchange of ideas and best practices by leaders in the field of athlete development. However, the history of PAADS has been primarily focused on professional athletic organizations, and it seems to be a collection of groups rather than an independent organization.

According to PAADS, Athlete Development Specialists (AD Specialists) are people who the casual sport fan likely never hears about, but are critical to sports organizations and teams. AD Specialists bring a wide range of diverse expertise while working directly with athletes and organizations to help ensure athletes are able to achieve optimal results not only while playing the sport, but outside of the sport as well. AD Specialists focus on creating opportunities for athletes to excel in their sport while mitigating the challenges and issues many aspiring elite or professional athletes face both during and after their playing careers. AD Specialists come from a wide range of educational backgrounds and athletic experiences. They hold degrees in Psychology, Business, Engineering, Social Work, Sports Management, and many other fields. AD Specialists are not all former professional athletes. Many have played high school or collegiate level athletics and some have never participated in elite level athletics. The organization believes the common denominator for successful AD Specialists is a desire to see athletes shine in all facets of their lives.

DEFINING A NAME

Assisting student and professional athletes outside of the sporting environment has been a challenge for many years. There is not a specific name for the industry or a blueprint for curriculum design, and there are no guidelines for practical application that focus on helping the student or professional athlete in the area of personal development. More importantly, there is a lack of investment from the industry regarding athletes' personal development.

One of the issues mentioned above is the lack of an industry name. Personal Development for athletes is currently called different things throughout the sporting community. Kim Durand, the Associate Athletic Director of Student Development for the University of Washington, agrees:

> Sometimes, I think we get wrapped up into the labels, but I think we are all trying to aim at the same thing. We may call it different things at different levels of sports, but the intent is to make sure athletes at all levels continue to grow and be productive inside and outside of the athletic arena. I think if we can bring them all together and worked together towards a goal, we will all be better off.[8]

According to PAADS, athlete development has different connotations to different people. For some, it is the development of specific athletic skills, while for others it is about turning athletes into better competitors. PAADS particularly defines athlete development as helping organizations and individuals develop the whole person in an athletic context. They care not only about helping the person excel athletically, but about ensuring these individuals are prepared and capable of achieving success outside of sport.

The mentioned groups working with athletes have collective and individual desired goals in the personal, social, and professional development of athletes. Key areas of focus include: life skills, student athlete engagement, student athlete leadership, and professional areas such as player development, player engagement, and the independent level of athlete development. A holistic approach, which is associated with sports participation, encompasses all of the above, resulting in Personal Player Development.

These three words: Personal, Player, and Development, supported by their individual definitions, represent the essence of much, if not all of the terms used today by college athletic departments, professional sports teams, and independent organizations when working with athletes.

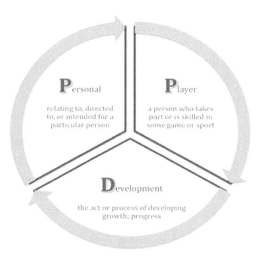

Figure 1.0 Industry Name, PPD

Personal is defined as relating to, directed to, or intended for a particular person. Player is defined as a person who takes part or is skilled in some game or sport. Development is defined as the act or process of developing; growth; progress.[9] Therefore, the industry should formally be defined as Personal Player Development (PPD). The phrase

37

PPD has a comprehensive approach to the personal development of athletes at all levels of sport and should be recognized as an industry, field of practice in its purest form.

PPD IS AN ART

Art is a diverse range of human activities, and the products of those activities.[10] Personal Player Development is described as the art of specifically focusing on the personal development of athletes, at all levels, for the sole purpose of allowing athletes to develop and maintain a healthy, positive, and balanced lifestyle. The diverse range of human activities associated with sports participation requires an approach that successfully understands and assists athletes' thoughts, feelings, and behavior.

To the practitioner, PPD can be seen as a scientific art, or a skill acquired by experience, study, or observation. Many of the individuals working with athletes in the area of PPD acquired their skill either through experience playing sports, observation of athletic behavior in sports, or in rare cases, have researched athletes and PPD. Although these three areas are each essential, an individual PPD expert should not be limited to just one realm of experience. An individual possessing all three traits provides any sports organization with a serious advantage. However, the current qualifications of PPD experts working in the field of athletics remain unknown.

Why is PPD so important to all of us? To universities or professional organizations, real PPD provides significant brand protection. For the coach, PPD assists in the overall performance of an athlete. For the parent, PPD is the essence of developing a child to become an adult. Finally, for the athlete, PPD allows them to develop a skill set in which they have rarely been exposed. Ultimately, it will prove valuable during and after their sporting experience. It is specifically important to understand athletic identity, decision-making, and coping skills as athlete's transition to the post-athletic phase of their lives.

ECHOING THE NEED

The growing need for PPD services is echoed by many professionals in the field of athletics today. Mary Ellen Leicht believes:

> Personal Player Development as it pertains to planning for a future outside of athletics, I feel is essential at all levels of collegiate athletics. Student athletes devote a tremendous amount of time and effort to perfecting their

athletic skills. There will come a time, and for some that's sooner than later, when sports will no longer play such a big role in their life. At that point, it's essential that plans have been put in place and decisions made that assist with that transition.[11]

Dr. William Broussard, the Athletic Director at Southern University, regards PPD as "extremely valuable." Dr. Broussard feels very few athletes have the maturity at age eighteen to succeed as well as we need them to in the classroom, on the field, and socially and states.

> PPD is needed in all areas for the student athlete. Individuals working with athletes daily across campuses in the United States and at various professional levels have been faced with the task of readjusting kids' egos, which often times have been distorted by the media, family, friends, rankings and the like. For some of us, we have been successful in readjusting their egos and helping student athletes become aware of the daunting possibilities of having a professional career. However, many student athletes appear to be so focused on playing professionally at the next level that in many ways they tune helping professionals out.[12]

The question must be asked: Do athletes tune helping professionals out, or is the message and method of delivery the issue?

Kevin Greene, a student athlete on the University of Southern California (USC) football team from 2009-2014, feels that "Athletes need PPD because we hold ourselves under a bubble, and we need to have assistance in just being a college athlete and developing while getting ready for life once sport is over."[13] Although Mr. Green admits that while at USC the department did not offer any seminars or workshops on the subject of PPD, he credits his overall support network in assisting him in graduating early as well as pushing him to pursue coursework at the graduate level.

On the professional level, we have at this point realized, that athletes still need personal development throughout most of their careers despite the amount of money that they earn. This is especially true since our current professional athletes in the signature sports are younger and wealthier than at any other time in the history of sports. Greg Taylor, the Senior Vice President of Player Development for the National Basketball

Association, believes "PPD is essential to the athlete. As we commit to developing the whole person, both the athlete and the non-athlete, Player Development and our commitment to respond to, as well as support, the players needs and challenges they face off the court is a really critical piece."[14]

According to Marviel Underwood, a former player for the Green Bay Packers, Denver Broncos, and Oakland Raiders:

> There is a definite need for someone to connect with the players and someone who has played sports and understands the issues, but [the question is] how to relate the message to players. To tell the truth, they have the rookie symposium, but we don't care about that. So it has to be something that carries through all season long, and they have to have sessions, mandatory for the first year players, and [they need to] ask players "what's your plan if the NFL does not work out?" It should be structured like school and college; these guys need to have a serious developmental plan.[15]

The problems and issues athletes at all levels face in our current society are not limited to race or gender. We are experiencing an athletic culture in which our athletes need a real personal development curriculum as well as applications and programs to ensure the proper personal development of athletes as complete individuals. Assistance for athletes ranges from avoiding serious trouble to making a healthy transition to the real world. In an era where there is a dedicated section titled "Sports Crime" in major publications such as the Huffington post, we can no longer ignore this growing problem.

According to Jocelyn Gebhardt, a former Lacrosse student athlete at East Stroudsburg University:

> You devote all of that time into your sport, but when it comes time to get help in the transition phase and networking or finding a job in your field, some of the coaches say, "good luck." If you have a dream to playing professional, they say, "Good luck, go out and do that." So if programs were in place to help athletes move forward and find that job or continue with sport related career goals, I think that would be excellent. PPD programs are

something that is missing and would be a piece of the puzzle.[16]

Over the past two decades, I have been able to interact with athletic directors, coaches, life skills coordinators, current and former high school players, parents, college and professional athletes as well as a host of individuals associated with PPD globally. Their response from interviews, surveys, educational-based research, practical application, athletic experience, and articles on the subject makes it clear that now, more than ever, our athletes require a serious approach toward their personal development.

Personal development needs to be interjected into athletes' daily routine, or we will continue to see negative effects such as low graduation rates, higher transfer rates, athletes involved in criminal activity, and an overall "troubled athlete." For example, if an athlete worked on his/her decision-making skills with the same dedication that she/he has worked on her/his jump shot, we would see a better athlete on and off the court. If an athlete were able to understand athletic identity as outlined in this text, they would have a better understanding of their role inside and outside of sport, making them a better athlete.

COLLEGE ATHLETIC DEPARTMENTS

Most college athletic departments have elements of PPD. Many of them have the same pattern of services offered such as: life skills, leadership development, career service, and community service. However, services and course programs to meet the total needs of student athletes are rarely offered. In fact, most athletes rarely take advantage of the services offered, mainly because they are voluntary, and one could argue not taking advantage of these services is the athletes' fault. Let's not forget the majority of athletes in college are still classified as teenagers, aged seventeen to nineteen, and services offered in personal development should be non-negotiable.

However, the main reason these services should be offered is intertwined in the rational for many athletes attending college in the first place. This reason is, has been, and always will be to play ball and ultimately become a professional player. Therefore, prior to offering services for athletes with the hope that they voluntarily participate, efforts should be made to understand delivery methods of personal player development and then interject other needed services such as career development, community service, and the like.

In a push to provide student athletes with the realities of achieving a professional career, colleges and universities invite motivational speakers to campus to address their athletes. Professionals should know by now that this concept has little impact. Hearing a speaker has minimal impact simply because athletes receive the 'rah rah' speech before every game and again at half time. Therefore, this type of motivation lasts about twenty minutes. Athletes today require an educational-based curriculum, seminars, workshops, and true personal development guidance, or the problems we are witnessing will only increase.

So much is being asked of the student athlete today and professionals need to reflect to determine if they are keeping up with the needs of these athletes. According to Kristy Belden, the Director of Player Development at the University of Central Florida:

> Having been a student-athlete and [having] worked in this business for thirteen years, I have been able to see what these kids are dealing with. This is a different society from years ago, and young men and women athletes need to have the resources for the issues they are being forced to deal with daily. I would also add the student-athlete today requires a holistic approach and not just the sport side and academic side; the development component has to be included. These students have to keep their fingers on a lot of things at once.[17]

If you are working in the field of athletics, ask yourself and your colleagues: What is the essence of athletic identity? The athlete's worldview? How have program courses been designed to aid in the personal development of the student athlete? Have programs been designed to address the stages of growth that athletes encounter along the athletic journey? How about understanding the transitional phases athletes encounter? More importantly, how athletes deal with these transitions? It is extremely difficult for helping professionals, regardless of ethnic background, to get to the core of developing the athlete without understanding the topics mentioned. This is not to say that there are not helping professionals making contributions to the development of the athlete. However, experience and research reveals that they often fall short in providing long-term developmental needs.

THE ACADEMIC RELATIONSHIP TO PPD

Most personnel assigned to work with athletes in the personal development arena either have experience playing sports on some level or have worked with athletes in some capacity. They bring their personal experience to the job and work from that point. From a historical perspective, this approach is acceptable. However, it does not mean they are particularly effective working with this population due to the academic and practical training needed to provide the necessary practical methods of application specifically for the athlete.

In reviewing academic disciplines, a variety of courses are offered for this generation than ever before. Courses in social media, hip-hop, and the other modern topics have been designed to reflect the need of the generation in front of us. Courses for the athlete, specifically on personal development, are virtually nonexistent. Why aren't we seeing a surge in courses offered to assist the intercollegiate discipline targeting personal development of the athlete? Graduate level disciplines such as counseling, sport management, and sport psychology have not developed courses designed with a comprehensive approach towards personal development of athletes.

When asked if Personal Player Development courses or a certificate focusing on PPD is needed, Dr. Howard Bartee, Jr., the Assistant Professor and Chair of Sports Administration at Belhaven University, responded, "I believe it is needed. We have individual courses that address PPD from a spiritual standpoint and Christian Worldview. Something as simple as tying a tie can be an asset to young athletes. Having a certificate, course or workshops for college student-athletes, I believe is important. I think that having PPD would be an asset to any program."[18]

Affirming Dr. Bartee's sentiment, Gary Darnell, who spent 37 years as a college football coach for eleven different universities, and is currently the American Football Coaches Association (AFCA) Associate Executive Director, reported, "I think there should be a baseline of what should be taught and the outcomes intended. Some people may emphasize matters of faith based on the institution. The schools are different from city to city, so one personal player development program won't fit all, but there should be a baseline."[19]

Therefore, if courses at the undergraduate and graduate level do not exist, how can we expect the people working with athletes under the PPD umbrella to properly assist in real personal development of the athletes within their care? On the collegiate level, personal development programs are being implemented. This is due to the mandated association bylaws. However, can they be effective if employees are not trained?

On a professional level there are very few, if any, programs targeting individuals working specifically on the personal development of athletes. The absence of personal development courses and training would explain why so many young collegiate athletes spend four years on a college campus or retire from a professional sport and still lack the necessary skills to make a significant contribution to our society.

Many athletic departments believe that having a sports psychologist on staff cures the personal development need. A sport psychologist role primarily focuses on performance enhancement as related to the sport. Sport psychologists help athletes become better athletes but not better people. According to Tom Ferraro, "pick up any text in sport psychology and you will have a very hard time finding any discussion at all about diagnosis or what the actual dynamics are inside the mind of athletes. Yes, these texts will offer some suppressive techniques on how to manage anxiety, anger, or lack of focus, but there will rarely, if ever, be commentary on typical diagnosis of athletes and the necessary psychotherapy. It would seem that everyone has decided to pretend that athletes have a lock on mental stability and just need a little pep talk and voila, all better.[20]

PPD FOUNDATION AND CURRICULUM DESIGN

Currently, the PPD structure is a combination of human resource services and contractors from a variety of fields. For example, some organizations, particularly at the professional level, design programs and bring in experts from their field to present on a topic to professional athletes. This is only beneficial if players are serious about receiving the information. Some professional players take full advantage of services offered while others enjoy the dream life as a professional athlete and postpone worrying about the future.

The introduced PPD foundation is built on three pillars: Personal, Social, and Professional. As seen in the table below, these three areas include a number of sub-groups, which comprise of the PPD curriculum. These sub-groups address the necessary areas to provide a successful approach towards personal development for athletes, specifically assisting them in their quest to either become a career professional or a professional athlete as well as live a healthy and balanced lifestyle.

The two PPD curriculum building blocks or topics, which hold all of the three pillars in place, are: Athletic Identity and Leadership, and the Decision Making Process. However, Athletic Identity is the starting point when working with athletes from all levels of sport if a widespread approach towards personal development is the main objective.

Table 1. PPD Foundation Topics and Sub-Groups

PPD Foundation and Sub-Groups		
Personal	Social	Professional
Athletic Identity	Athletic Identity	Athletic Identity
Relationship Issues, fatherhood, Motherhood role, family ties	Cultural Competency and Inclusion	Career Exploration and Guidance from start to finish
Health and wellness, during and after sport participation	Casual Relationship Development	Image and Brand development and protection
The Spirituality and the Athlete	The Justice System and Athletes	Network and Media Development
Money Management	Fan Appreciation	Education: Academic and Professional Programs
Leadership and the Decision Making Process	Leadership and the Decision Making Process	Leadership and the Decision Making Process

The PPD curriculum topics listed in the table above should be implemented by athletic organizations, and the individual colleges should start developing their own curriculum within this framework. The time is now, and the need has never been greater.

PPD SECTOR CHALLENGES

The PPD industry is dedicated to personal development for members of the global athletic community. This book will serve as a learning resource for all in the PPD industry. The PPD industry, including services on college campuses and within professional organizations, is relatively young and has a lot of growing to do as each generation of athletes are bringing new challenges every year.

There are four main sectors of PPD as seen in the following table. Each sector faces challenges pertaining to the implementation of a holistic PPD program. The high school, college, professional, and independent sectors all need a curriculum based program much like a sequence in math, history, or foreign language. If you think about it, a student starts off in basic math long before they enter trigonometry. Therefore, it is only fitting that PPD programs should be structured for the lowest learner and gradually grow in content.

PPD GATE KEEPERS AND THE MISINFORMED

The underlining reason PPD programs, courses, and related activities have not been fully embraced by the athletic community as a whole is because of the perspective of three unique groups. The youth sector parents and coaches, college head coaches, and professional organizations do not see a benefit to their main personal or organizational goal, which is to generate revenue or win games. The most significant pioneer of implementing PPD components with his team was the late 49er football coach, Bill Walsh. However, why should personal development of athletes begin once an athlete reaches millionaire status? Also, what is the fate of the thousands of athletes who never make it to the professional level? These athletes deserve an opportunity to personally develop.

Table 2. PPD Sector Challenges

PPD Sector Challenges

PPD Sectors	Sector Challenges
PPD Challenges on the High School Level	Parents and family buy-in Head coaches buy-in Awareness of the need to have PPD programs and services regardless of athletic potential Developing a high school curriculum Trained staff working with athletes Funding and implementation of a PPD
PPD Challenges on the Collegiate Level	Head coaches buy-in Funding PPD programs and services Develop a college curriculum Trained staff working with athletes Funding and implementation of a PPD
PPD Challenges on the Professional Level	Players buy-in Long-term curriculum based programming and development Trained staff working with athletes Youth level PPD investment Service to non-vested athletes
Independent	Head coaches buy-in Agents buy-in Players buy-in Ability to follow a designed curriculum Investment in training in PPD Establishing a network while building credibility

THE YOUTH LEVEL

The youth sports world is a booming business. Parents invest thousands of dollars on participation fees, hotels, flights, rental cars, and food just to see their child compete in the sport. Unlike previous generations, today's youth are deciding early on what their sport of choice is, and they are sticking to that sport.

Kids start playing as early as the second grade, and in many cases, they play the same sport year-round. Although medical research is clear regarding the necessary rest and recovery needed to aid in a child's development, year-round sport has become the norm. Since parents are predominately the driving force for youth athletic participation, there is an obvious question to be asked: Do parents value PPD the same way they value sport participation?

Other important questions to be considered are:

> How much PPD is required at the youth level of sport?
> What are the necessary components needed in the field of PPD?
> Are we providing a pathway or delivery methods at the youth level in PPD?

The likely place for PPD on the youth level would be at home with parents, in schools, and during youth camps, day clinics, and elite level exposure tournaments. I have attended AAU and youth sporting events for the past decade, and there is virtually no PPD taking place on the youth level. This would in part explain the growing number of behavioral problems we continue to witness in the athletic community.

Many would argue that parents should be teaching their kids some of the core fundamentals of PPD and in part, I would agree. However, considering the amount of information afforded to parents as it pertains to understanding the athletic culture, in combination with the amount of time a child spends with their parent(s) on a daily basis, the responsibility of teaching core elements of PPD on the youth level should rest predominately on middle and high school officials and coaches, but we know this is not the case.

High school athletes spend up to twelve hours on campus studying and engaged in sport-related activities. The high school athletic department has the largest student participation than any other activity on campus. Many of the sports are reported on regularly in the local paper and top level sponsored high school websites. The high school signature sports usually charge a fee at the gate, are being sponsored by apparel companies, and have games televised nationally. Our young student-athletes are involved in a college farm system which provides little information on the personal development of athletes.

Currently, state education standards do not include PPD as a necessity for the athlete because it is not part of the standard curriculum. Therefore, teachers at the high school level have little time to focus on the topic of PPD because they must cover the state standards in preparation for state exams. Also, teachers have little influence over the athlete outside of the required course work.

Youth level sports have a high demand for PPD services, but only a few professionals in the United States focus on this targeted audience for a variety of reasons. One assumed reason is the pushback PPD professionals would receive from parents regarding PPD services. In the absence of research on this topic, it has historically been difficult to decipher how parents really feel about PPD, and if they see value in PPD services for their kids.

In a random survey of over 100 parents attending the Jam On It AAU basketball tournament in Reno Nevada (2013), they were asked their opinion about PPD and the youth athlete. According to tournament director Matt Williams, the Jam On It AAU tournament is the largest AAU basketball tournament in the world. In 2013, the tournament hosted over 1,100 teams ranging from second grade to the twelfth grade. Questions and responses can be seen below:

1. How would you rate this event?
Great — 44%
Pretty Good — 40%
Good — 16%
Not Good At All — 0%

2. What is the goal for you and your child through basketball participation?
Enjoy sports — 16%
Get an athletic scholarship — 16%
Make the high school team — 24%
All of the above — 44%

3. Do you think personal development is just as important as skill development?
Yes — 100%
No — 0%

4. If the event had a PPD component would you encourage your child to attend?

Yes — 80%
No — 12%
Maybe — 8%

5. If the event had a PPD component targeting parents would you attend?

Yes — 68%
No — 32%
Maybe — 0%

The results from the survey indicates that 100% of parents believe PPD is just as important as skill development at the youth level, and 80% of parents would encourage their child to attend a PPD related event. Christopher Thomas, a Nike SPARQ (SPARQ is an acronym for: Speed, Power, Agility, Reaction, and Quickness) Master Basketball Trainer, believes:

> PPD needs to start when a kid decides they want to stop playing other sports and focus on one sport. When we decide to interject it at the pro level, in a rookie orientation it's too late. Which means someone at the next level has to do a lot more work in the personal development area. PPD completes the athletes' package; PPD is as necessary to the athlete as is regeneration and recovery for an athlete. There is so much that goes on between getting ready for a game and during a season. Coach doesn't like me, why am I not ranked, I should be ranked higher, blah, blah, blah. People don't realize there is so much that goes into being a basketball player off the court, and these kids at all levels need assistance in this business.[21]

THE HEAD COACH

Unfortunately, at the collegiate level, a head coach's job is predicated on wins and losses. Coaching in college is a high stress environment and according to Adam Kramer, it is important to "win at all cost, win now, or you might not have a chance to win later, win football games, or you're fired. Ensure that your players are eligible to play, and if they are, make sure they're physically and mentally prepared. For head college football coaches, it's that simple."[22] He continues by asking, "Just how much responsibility does (or should) a coach have for a player's academic performance, social activities and failures outside the football field? Where does that part of his job both start and stop?"[23]

The biggest problem for coaches in PPD is trust. Most of the coaches do not trust the fact that PPD for their athlete would result in a better athlete and more wins. The lack of belief in PPD is really a lack of understanding of what PPD is and how PPD can help a coach win a conference championship or a national championship. Therefore, providing PPD services from a coach's perspective is a waste of time. Leadership and team chemistry are topics important to coaches, and until the personal development of athletes becomes a mandate from governing bodies of sport, our athletes are left facing a difficult task in the area of personal development if left up to the head coach.

Jeff Janssen believes:

> A lot of the big time coaches and the big time programs are solely or primarily rewarded for winning. A lot of times the other aspects are certainly considered nice, but obviously a coach's job mostly depends upon whether or not he or she is winning. Until some of the reward structures start rewarding some of the things outside of winning, it is still going to be an issue. I think PPD is huge; it is one of those areas often overlooked by a lot of different people. It is important to really focus in on the PPD aspects. A lot of times people assume that great athletes have PPD skills, but in a lot of cases they may not, the environment makes it easy to sometimes adopt an entitled approach to what athletes are doing. So, I think PPD is definitely important.[24]

Embracing PPD for coaches is an added benefit and can be considered a missing ingredient for success. For a coach, PPD could be the difference between winning 50% of his games to winning 80% of his games and graduating a higher percentage of athletes. According to Jamil Northcutt, the Assistant Athletic Director for Internal Operations at Ole Miss, benefits of investing in PPD "would include better services for student-athletes, coaches, and administrators. The surrounding community would also benefit and we would have a more prepared student-athlete. We would also have more wins on the field, increased job placement for athletes, decrease in off field distractions, increased prestige of the institution and increased in morale of athletics staff and professionals."[25]

A true PPD staff member is the much-needed soundboard for players, a person who can assist athletes in areas that the head or assistant coaches either have no time for, or simply are not trained for. The question is: Do coaches really care about the personal development of athletes, or are they using the athletes to reach their own personal goals? "If you look at the reward structure and the penalty structure, these two explain why we are still seeing some of these issues. There is not total alignment between what people are professing they say (is important), to what they are actually rewarding monetarily, in terms of what is important."[26]

The Positive Coaching Alliance as well as educational courses for coaches on the topic of character building, misses the mark regarding personal development of athletes. Do we really expect coaches to have the ability to deliver PPD exercises when their jobs are to win games? No coach in America, especially football coaches, can be the jack-of-all-trades. Understanding this, football coaches have an assistant coach for offense, defense, special teams, running backs, receivers and a number of other positions. If head coaches could do everything, they would not need all of these coaches to assist them.

Having a qualified PPD professional on staff as well as a complete PPD program, makes the coach's job easier. As a former Division 1 coach, and current college basketball color commentator and studio analyst for ESPN, Dan Dakich speaks on the need for a PPD staff member:

> Absolutely have somebody that is qualified and can relate to these kids. I saw the need for this years ago. There has been a transformation in how we can relate to these athletes. When I first started, we had no social media, but now college sports and the athletes that play are so much bigger because access to media outlets are in the palm of your hand.
>
> Google can kill ya when a coach has to worry about what athletes are saying and doing; it takes away from the coach doing their job, and that's where a PPD staff person can play a big role in managing all of the off the court or field stuff. If I ever went back into coaching, I would make sure I hire a PPD person just to work with my guys on the development side of things. Social, behavioral,

relationship issues, you name it; that person would deal with it. Hell, I would bring you (Dr. Robinson) in to work with these guys.[27]

According to Lamonte Winston the Director of Player Engagement for the Oakland Raiders:

If I show athletes and coaches we have programs that will help athletes address the difficulties of life. The pressure of the job, of not having a job, of birth, of death, of divorce, of drugs and alcohol. All of the things that are involved, you are going to have a more productive person, you will have a more productive player, you have a more productive student. For example, you may have a student coming from a real financially challenged and underprivileged environment, but if you have some resources that can help him/her transition to this beautiful campus, that is totally different from where they grew up. The kid that grows up fatherless, if you have staff that can talk about helping the athlete transition without a father.

As a coach, you need to have someone on staff to do everything possible, so you can be in front of all the issues that students and professional athletes bring to campus or to an organization. So the return on investment is all [of]those things. I want a better athlete; I want a better student athlete; I want a better pro; I want a better performer on Sunday or Saturday or Monday. Another example, if Mark is on my team, and he is having marital issues or relationship problems, and we are going to play a four game swing or have two games in a week, as a coach I want to know that we have the resources to help Mark with his family [and] with his marital issue. Not providing those resources could be the difference between Mark scoring his average 20 points a game, or Mark scoring 10 points a game. If this happens we have problems.[28]

The Walsh Way

Many coaches in today's sports world forget that the late, great, Bill Walsh used Dr. Harry Edwards' expertise for many years. Dr. Edwards has been a consultant with the 49ers organization since 1985. According to Dr. Edwards:

> I was part of a generation that routinely played multiple sports in both high school and college. After arriving in California from E. St. Louis to play football at USC in 1960, I found that I was severely deficient academically. I was directed to Fresno City College (a "feeder school" for USC) where I matriculated for one semester while playing basketball and track (I set a National discus record in May of 1960).
>
> I subsequently took a basketball/track grant-in-aid to San Jose State University (Fresno was the hottest place I'd ever lived, and I had no intention of staying any longer than necessary.) I ultimately graduated with honors from San Jose State (in 3-1/2 years), earned a Woodrow Wilson Fellowship, and a Cornell University Fellowship to Cornell in 1964, fellowships that I took rather than enter the NFL with the Minnesota Vikings or the AFL with the San Diego Chargers. (Though I never played football in college, at 6'8", 260 lbs with a "brutal" game of basketball, I nonetheless attracted a lot of football interest, but my fellowships paid more - simple as that). Here is the rest of my journey.[29]

Years later, Dr. Edwards became a consultant on issues of diversity for all three major sports. He was hired by the Commissioner of Major League Baseball in 1987 to help with efforts to increase front office representation of minorities and women in baseball. He was also with the Golden State Warriors of the NBA from 1987 through 1995, specializing in player personnel counseling and programs. The programs and methods he developed for dealing with the issues and challenges facing professional football player personnel were adopted by the entire NFL in 1992. The NFL also adopted the Minority Coaches Internship and Outreach Program that he developed with Coach Bill Walsh at the San Francisco Forty Niners in 1986.[30] To date, there has not been another person to make such a large contribution to the personal development of professional athletes after Dr. Edwards. While Dr. Edwards has been influential in the movement of personal development for athletes, his contributions have for the most part, been individually focused. His contributions to the industry, and the helping professionals who desire to assist athletes, have gone unnoticed and missed the mark in helping millions of athletes.

Bill Walsh and Dr. Edwards' collaboration seemed to be ahead of their time as it pertained to understanding the needs of players on the collegiate and professional level. This new generation of coaches, the win at all cost group, could learn valuable personal player development lessons from Bill Walsh's techniques and tactics.

The PPD industry has been identified and developed because we, as a sporting community, have become obsessed with winning, earning a profit, and skill development. We have placed so much emphasis on the bottom line and return on investment, that we have neglected the personal development needs of the individuals responsible for winning and earning the profit: the athletes. The achievements of pioneers like Coach Walsh and Dr. Edwards must be recognized and applauded, but the time has come for the industry of PPD to move in a direction that will benefit athletes from all sports, socioeconomic backgrounds, and genders.

CHAPTER THREE

ATHLETIC IDENTITY

Everyone who competes in the games goes into strict training. They do it to get a crown that will not last, but we do it to get a crown that will last forever [1 Corinthians 9:25]

A MULTI-DIMENSIONAL CONCEPT

Athletic identity is an area of study we know little about, specifically as influenced by personal growth and development, in relation to other disciplines being studied throughout the globe. Athletes are a vital part of our daily activities, conversations, and business. Parents, the media, education, and professional sports all play a unique role in defining who a person competing in sports thinks that he or she is. An athlete's often hidden vulnerabilities; the paradox of the invincible and the invisible, are all phenomenally linked to the concept of athletic identity.

The amount of revenue associated with the performance of athletes is increasing. The pressure to win placed on coaches and athletes, the importance of athletic facilities, and the protection of institutional brands are essential in high school and college athletics. Governing bodies, athletic associations, and the United States Olympic Committee could benefit from investing in alternative methods to assist in the personal growth of the athlete.

With the exception of the PPD curriculum introduced in the previous chapter, currently there is not a uniformed basic curriculum, program, or approach that aids in the understanding of an athlete's personal growth and development using athletic identity as a major building block. Unlike graduation rates as well as transfer and retention rates. The area of personal growth for the athlete has lagged behind the importance of other priorities such as facility development and sponsorship. Therefore, investing in athletic identity of the student athlete is in many cases a low priority mainly due to the difficulty in actually measuring how and when growth occurs.

Most institutional programs involving or assisting athletes that are endorsed or sanctioned by the National Federation for High School (NFHS), and the National Collegiate Athletic Association (NCAA) focus on sport development education for coaches, and do not mention athletic identity. At one time, the NCAA established the *CHAMPS/Life Skills* program as a model for assisting in the personal growth of student athletes, but it also failed to include athletic identity. However, that program has gone through a change, and its future appears to be uncertain. The governing bodies of two of the largest sporting organizations have no clue about the relationship between student athletes and athletic identity which is shocking. The countless number of athletes that have stories directly related to athletic identity have gone virtually unnoticed by governing bodies.

Kirk Dixo, a former student athlete states that:

> As a high school athlete I was proud of earning all-state honors and being recruited at a D-I level, earning the scholarship, earning a starting spot, lettering four years, and eventually being named captain in a varsity sport my senior year. It was a lot of work, lots of hours balancing my school, sport, social activities, and a part-time job in the off-season. To succeed, I was consumed with my sport because it required a structured schedule, and the discipline to make responsible choices to hold it all together. In essence, my whole life and identity revolved around my sport. Others in my life were consumed with my role too (like family and close friends who came to home games, traveled to away games, and scheduled vacation and time off around our playing season).[31]

Dixo's story is an echo of millions of athletes who have participated in sports and received little to no help in finding out who they are after sport participation.

TRADITIONAL ATHLETIC IDENTITY

Heavy demands of the athletic role conflict with other important roles and activities in such a way that problems for the athlete arise concerning limited peer relationships, lack of career and social development opportunities, and restricted self-concept and basis for self-worth. It has been suggested that many student athletes either lack the time or interest to undertake career planning or view such an endeavor as a threat to their athletic identity and their dream of being a professional athlete.[32] Therefore, it appears athletic identity is closely related to career adjustment and transformation from sports to a career.

In an attempt to understand athletic identity and provide a model to assist in problematic areas of concern as mentioned above, one first has to review the definition of athletic identity and to accept the fact that there are different types of athletes. The Athletic Identity Model (AIM) developed by Brewer, Van Raalte, and Linder (1993), offers a framework to identify the different levels at which a person can identify being an athlete. Brewer et al., defines athletic identity as the degree to which an individual identifies with the athlete role. The key word in their definition is **individual**. However, the AIM is limited in key areas if the original intent was to promote personal growth and development for athletes.

According to Galloway (2007), AIM provides a basic method to assess how strongly an individual identifies with the athlete role. Unfortunately, the researchers did not specifically identify if or how people transition from one construct to the others. In agreement with Galloway, further research is needed to determine how this model develops over time to define the common characteristics for individuals at each construct, to determine if this model is linear, and to identify potential effects of ethnicity and gender on this model.

The Brewer et al. model is lacking definitions and guidelines for the athlete identification categories as well as a progressive direction to a healthy and balanced human developmental process. Examining the external factors to determine if an athlete identifies as a non-athlete, a recreational/fitness athlete, an intramural athlete, or an intercollegiate/national athlete is informative, but is not a construct needed for personal development.

Galloway focuses on research questions and issues that must be given consideration and attention when undertaking research in athletic identity. Such questions include:

➢ What characteristics do individuals in each construct exhibit?
➢ What is the need for reporting on the correlation of ethnicity and athlete identity?
➢ What is athletic identity and what are cross-cultural implications?
➢ How do athletes of various sports identify with the model?

In agreement with Galloway, additional questions regarding the psychology of athletes as well as counseling methods applicable for the black athlete are areas that need to be further investigated.

THE NEED FOR A CLOSER LOOK AT ATHLETIC IDENTITY

Understanding the thoughts, feelings, and behaviors of athletes remains somewhat of a mystery to many who work with athletes as well as the fans who admire them. Why would an athlete making millions of dollars commit a crime? Why does an athlete on a full scholarship get kicked off the team for poor behavior? Why do so many of our athletes today have egos so large that they disrespect the coach or spiral out of control after retiring from the sport? How and what methods of application best work with athletes in dealing with the pressures of sports participation?

The sports media and professionals specializing in non-athletic related areas often give their perspective on athlete behavior. Often, they are far from understanding athletic behavior. In fact, many individuals working with athletes daily do not understand the dynamics involving athletic behavior and shy away from the conversation regarding athletic behavior completely.

According to Greg Bishop of the New York Times, the divorce rate for NFL players is between 60 and 80 percent. This is higher than that of the general population where nearly half of marriages end in divorce, but it is comparable to athletes in other sports (2009). What Bishop fails to provide is a rationale for this high divorce rate for athletes. Tim Elmore believes that the biggest reason athletes find themselves in trouble is Abandonment Abundance (2012). He continues, "What troubled athletes need is a coach, teacher, or leader who makes appropriate demands and sets appropriate standards for them in a responsive environment of belief and concern. In short, they need us to display a balance of two qualities—they need them to be both responsive and demanding." [33]

Elmore agrees that troubled athletes are an unfortunate reality of working with any sports team. He is well known for his work in the area of leadership and the next generation, not specifically understanding the behavior of athletes. As the athlete is in many ways different from the non-athlete, applications and discussions should be completely separate.

A report by Pete Thamel and Greg Bedard in the magazine, *Sports Illustrated* discusses Aaron Hernandez's, a former NFL player for the New England Patriots, questionable behavior in 2013. "The marijuana use and gang concerns worried some NFL teams immensely," they wrote. NFL general managers do not make moral judgments. They make calculated choices. They know from decades of experience, that a lot of athletes cannot make the jump to a pro lifestyle, because they don't want to make the jump. They want to take their lifestyle to the pros. The question of investigative reporting should focus on why athletes want to bring their lifestyle to the pros. Instead, the article, like many others, is filled with more questions than answers.[34]

According to Kelly Jordan Diener, the Assistant Athletic Director for Student Services at the University of Wisconsin-Milwaukee:

So many people do not think about it or talk about it [athletic identity]. Athletic identity is only discussed once athletes are finished. It's an important conversation for people to have, and we don't talk about it. I heard a saying "don't waste a good injury." Athletic identity is something student athletes don't understand and injuries as well as other elements shape phases of athletic identity. Most student-athletes love being student athletes and athletic identity is a very important topic to discuss.[35]

THE PPD PARADIGM FOR ATHLETIC IDENTITY

The process of shaping one's athletic identity is the missing link in program development as well as practical application when working with athletes on most levels. This missing link has been absent because research in the area of athletic identity has not introduced a paradigm that has been able to explain the factors associated with a developmental process of the athlete as it pertains to how the athlete's psyche, or worldview, is shaped due to sports participation.

The athlete's worldview in this paradigm consists of his/her thoughts, feelings, and behavior, specifically surrounding sports participation. When we dismiss the worldview of an athlete from a personal development stand point, we are immediately at a disadvantage in the helping relationship with athletes. This is simply because we are unaware of a starting and ending point in the personal developmental process. In many cases, helping professionals use a number of ineffective methods, or no methods at all, to assist in true personal development or growth.

The worldview of the athlete is also multi-dimensional, and the associated factors shaping an athlete's worldview may not be the exact same for other athletes. Although the specific ideology of the athlete's worldview is multi-dimensional, the starting point or shaping of the worldview is similar for all athletes.

According to Chris Herren, a former basketball player founder of the company *Hoop Dreams*, and author of *Basketball Junkie: A Memoir*:

Most athletes are left untreated. Every kid that steps on campus has a story, and that story needs to be told. I tell every college administration I sit in front of that you have weight-lifting, study hall, tutors, etc., but you're lacking in the wellness component to help athletes with the specific emotional and spiritual aspects that will help athletes. When these kids come to campus with baggage, they need help then, but athletes don't get noticed until they fail a drug test, so schools are mainly active, not proactive.[36]

This paradigm of athletic identity has been developed to assist in understanding athletes' worldview from the beginning stages of sport participation through the exit phases of the sports journey. This is true regardless of the athletes' level, including middle school through professional sport participation. The paradigm of athletic identity also assists in understanding the rationale behind the exit, such as injury, graduation, academic defeat, etc.

Understanding an athlete's worldview, although important, is significantly different from altering an athlete's worldview which is the unique benefit to the PPD athletic identity paradigm. The paradigm also provides methods of application to assist the athlete and helping professionals in providing a holistic approach to developing the athlete from a personal, social, and professional developmental standpoint.

Unlike the Brewer et al. Athletic Identity Model[37], which lacks definitions and guidelines for the athlete identity categories as well as a progressive direction to a healthy and balanced human developmental process, the PPD athletic identity model has defined guidelines. It includes athletic identity categories, and a progressive direction towards a healthy and balanced developmental process.

Some practitioners may connect the PPD athletic identity rationale and methods of application to Cognitive Behavior Therapy (CBT). CBT is a type of psychotherapeutic treatment that helps patients understand the thoughts and feelings that influence behaviors. CBT is commonly used to treat a wide range of disorders including: phobias, addiction, depression, and anxiety.[38] The difference between the PPD athletic identity and CBT is that athletic identity is directly related to sport participation and has been researched using athletes. Therefore, all associated treatable disorders identified in CBT as they may relate to athletic identity are a result of a number of contributing factors due to sport involvement.

Additionally, CBT is generally short-term and focused on helping clients deal with a very specific problem. During the course of treatment, people learn how to identify and change destructive or disturbing thought patterns that have a negative influence on behavior. The PPD athletic identity concept is designed to assist in social, personal, and professional growth using the positive athletic related factors to assist athletes in personal growth.

The PPD athletic identity paradigm was constructed using years of research and practical application with athletes across the globe. Athletes from different genders, socioeconomic status, ethnic and cultural differences, ages, and multiple variations of parental status were included in the research. The athletic identity paradigm construct also stems from countless numbers of interviews from helping professionals in the independent athlete development sectors as well as higher education athletic representatives from a variety of institutions.

THE PPD ATHLETIC IDENTITY MODEL

Athletic identity is one of the two supporting pillars of the PPD curriculum foundation, as discussed in the previous chapter. The other supporting pillar is the area of leadership, and the decision making process. Athletic identity is a multi-dimensional concept consisting of a developmental model with personal, social, and professional components that ultimately shape the progressive stages of athletic identity.

Athletes have a unique opportunity to experience a multitude of life developing events, exercises, and interactions with people simply because they can play a sport and more importantly are identified as an athlete. Therefore, athletic identity in the PPD industry is defined as "the level of maturity and understanding an athlete has in his/her efforts to maximize opportunities."

Athletic identity is defined as such for two reasons. First, it is so that we can admit that an athlete's status in sport or on a team can change at any given time which would affect the athlete's identity instantly. Secondly, the longer an individual participates in a sport, the more they will identify with the role of the athlete. Thus, having the maturity to maximize opportunities while you are in the role of the athlete is crucial for personal, social, and professional development. This is true mainly because athletes are limited to the amount of time they have in identifying with the athlete role. For example, some athletes play high school sports and never make it as an athlete at the collegiate level, while others who compete on the collegiate level never make it to the ranks of professional. Therefore, the amount of time allotted to athletes, specifically in competition, is predicated on athletic ability.

To many athletes, athletic identity is a feeling of ***invincibility*** resulting in the inability to identify, understand, desire, and resolve issues and problems for the athlete associated with the athletic experience. This is largely due to a lack of meaningful information about an athlete's unique worldview associated with sport participation. Therefore, we continue to engage with athletes and act as if the issues surrounding their worldview are ***invisible***.

Athletic identity is ***invincible*** in that athletes cannot escape the effects of athletic participation and simultaneously ***invisible,*** because helping professionals have failed to recognize or accept that understanding the worldview of the athlete is necessary.

Through research and experience, it has become clear that many of the associated problems athletes face, as outlined previously in Table 2: PPD Sector Challenges, are not solely due to their ethnic background, but are influenced by the athletic culture they find themselves in. With that said, the problems athletes from different ethnic backgrounds face vary in many ways.

As reported by Lois Arbogast, Strategic Communications Consultant with DRT Strategies:

> The biggest adjustment for me was finding a way to still identify with the athlete I'd worked so hard to become, while accepting that the professional version of me was what was going to provide over the years. I'm now five years out from graduating, and I feel like I've finally found a way to be both people. The struggle for me was [that] I felt as if I had to be all or nothing, one or the other, when ultimately I can be both.[39]

Regardless of the ethnic make-up, socioeconomic background, grade level, or gender of an individual athlete with dreams of competing at the highest level, each will undoubtedly experience problems associated with the sports culture. How we move to combat and limit the problems within the sports culture as it relates to athletic identity is critical to the future success of our athletes. Specifically, it is important to focus on how these potential problems affect productively in competition, and more importantly, after exiting the sport. Every athlete should be ready and able to look forward to the next phase of life's journey.

According to Dave Crowder, co-founder and partner at a venture capital and private equity firm:

> Post graduation, I remember no one recognized me, or introduced me, or invited me to speak like they used to. Looking back, I know my image or what I thought of myself (what I thought others thought of me) was in many ways an ego thing on my part, but when I sat in business staff meetings in my first job and looked around the table, the fact that no one knew what it took to compete at that

level of sport, or even cared about it as value, well it used
to choke me up. It became "a hole in my soul."[40]

Like many athletes that graduate, Dave Crowder and Lois Arbogast
both encountered issues adjusting to life after sport participation. These
scenarios present a question: What did the university do to assist them in
the developmental process while they were competing? As mentioned in
chapter two, athletic departments bring in guest speakers to discuss the
latest trends, buzzwords, and hot topics. Trainings covering subjects like
social media and leadership may look good on paper, but they only
scratch the surface of what athletes really need to learn about themselves
and the sports culture in order to have a holistic experience. In addition
to narrow topics, in most cases, there is little to no follow-up from these
sessions by the speakers, severely limiting the potential for any long-term
effectiveness. If an athletic department brings in a social media expert to
address the dangers and benefits of social media, what exactly does the
follow-up look like? The rules regarding social media for an athlete are
clear: do not post or say anything that could be seen or taken as negative
about anyone or anything. It's that simple. However, follow-up is still
needed to guide athletes on how to use social media to their advantage,
both during and post-sport, to build their brand, network, and to develop
a professional presence online.

Individuals working or participating in athletics have a unique
dedication to the sports culture. This dedication, regardless of role, is
found in few other fields due to the vast time invested in one particular
environment. In grades K-12, the most participated activity on the planet
is the participation in sports other than academics.

The age of entry into sport culture mirrors our educational system,
but it differs in that sports participation is voluntary. Through this
voluntary act or commitment, perceptions regarding thoughts, feelings,
and behavior are developed. This helps to define how individuals
involved in sports culture view the world around them; this is known as
the athlete's worldview.

ATHLETIC IDENTITY AND DEVELOPING THE
WORLDVIEW OF THE ATHLETE

In our efforts to better understand athletic identity, one must examine
the academic stages and the sport related factors associated with shaping
an athlete's worldview. Factors such as sport related entitlement,
entitlement contributors, time, and time verse time management are core

factors that shape an athlete's worldview. The term worldview, also called Weltanschauung in German, is defined as:

1) The overall perspective from which one sees and interprets the world, and
2) A collection of beliefs about life and the universe held by an individual or a group.[41]

Academic and professional stages such as K-12, college, professional sports, and the post athletic stage are independent areas that affect the overall developmental and worldview belief for athletes in the area of athletic identity.

Personal Player Development nurtures athletes through the academic related stages and the sport related factors. These areas can shape the athlete's worldview, and are important components where growth can take place as well as areas that can be measured. Therefore, when examining athletic identity, we need to consider how athletic identity is formed using the Athletic Identity Worldview Formation Model (AIWFM), as seen in Figure 2. This shaping process or model has multiple dimensions with a variety of proposed outcomes to an athlete's worldview. The beauty of the AIWFM is that it can lead to the personal development and growth of the athlete.

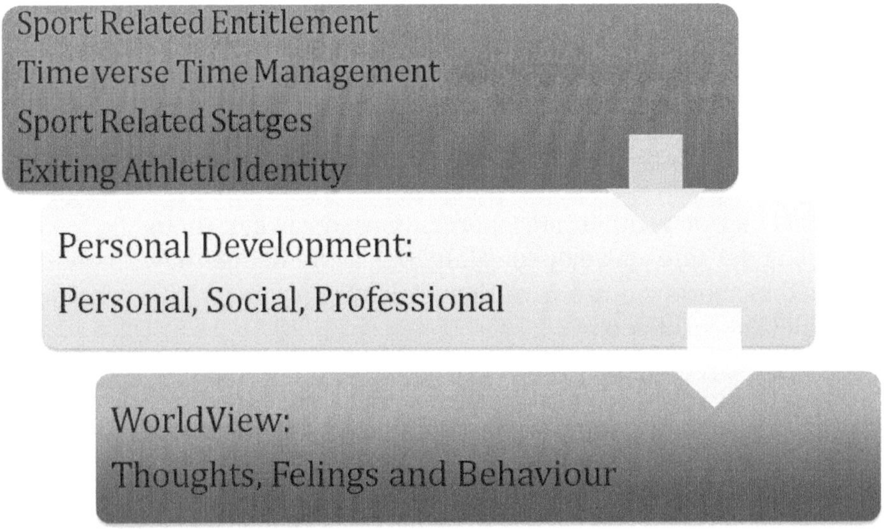

Sport Related Entitlement
Time verse Time Management
Sport Related Statges
Exiting Athletic Identity

Personal Development:
Personal, Social, Professional

WorldView:
Thoughts, Felings and Behaviour

Figure 2. Athletic Identity Worldview Formation Model [AIWFM]

The academic related stages of athletic identity include the academic year of the athlete and a likely list of challenging factors associated with sport participation during that time, as seen in Table 3. Also during this time sport related entitlement contributors are at work, as outlined in Table 4. The combination of academic related stages and the entitlement contributors play a major role in shaping the worldview of the athlete. Although athletic ability does play a factor to a certain extent, initially it is the input and work of the entitlement contributors at the early stages, which override athletic ability.

Sport Challenges

Sport Related Stages	*Entitlement Contributors*
Elementary/ Middle School	• *Time* • *Parents and family* • *Teachers* • *Youth sport participation* • *Social media*
Post Athletic 1	• *Time* • *Parents, family, and friends* • *Social media*
High School and College	• *Time* • *Parents and family* • *Friends* • *Sports participation* • *Social media* • *Teachers, staff, and alumni* • *Sports travel* • *The recruitment process* • *Media coverage* • *The de-recruitment process* • *Community and law enforcement* • *Free apparel* • *Agents* • *Groupies*
Post Athletic 2	• *Time* • *Parents, family, and friends* • *Social media* • *Work colleagues* • *Agent* • *Sycophants and groupies*

Professional	• **Time**
	• **Parents and family**
	• **Friends**
	• **Sports participation (Pro level)**
	• **Social media**
	• **Sports travel**
	• **Sponsorship and endorsements**
	• **Media coverage**
	• **Community and law enforcement**
	• **Free apparel**
	• **Sycophants and groupies**
Post Athletic 3	• **Time**
	• **Parents, family, and friends**
	• **Work colleagues**
	• **Social media**
	• **Agent**
	• **Sycophants and groupies**

Table 3. Sport Related Stages and Entitlement Contributors

SPECIFIC CHALLENGES FOR ATHLETES

As seen in the Table 4, athletes at all levels of experience face a number of challenges associated with sport participation. Stress, anxiety, loneliness, and depression are not isolated to athletes; however, we must also consider that sports were originally established as a recreational activity. Over time, we began to view sport in many ways as a tool or remedy to stress, anxiety, loneliness and depression. We currently live in a society where sports are not the cure, but it is established as an activity that produces specific sports related illnesses. The relationship with athletes and social media is undoubtedly a major contributor to the above sport related illnesses. Pleasing coaches, parents, and peers for the athlete, particularly on the youth level through the college ranks, is a largely unnoticed phenomenon. Due to the nature of the various demands on an athlete, these athletes neglect non-sport related activities and tend to dedicate unnecessary time to sport development and participation.

Academic and Athletic Stages, and Challenges

Academic and Athletic Stages	**Problems Associated With Sport Culture**
Middle and High School	**Stress** **Anxiety** **Loneliness** **Depression** **Social media (fear of missing out)** **Expectations** **Need to please coach parents and family** **Neglect of non-sport related activities** **Dedicated time to the sport**
College	**Stress** **Anxiety** **Loneliness** **Depression** **Social media (fear of missing out)** **Expectations** **Need to please coach parents and family** **Neglect of non-sport related activities** **Dedicated time to the sport**
Professional	**Stress** **Anxiety** **Loneliness** **Depression** **Social media (fear of missing out)** **Expectations** **Pressure to support parents and family** **Neglect of non-sport related activities** **Isolation because of the sport**
Post Athletic	**Stress** **Anxiety** **Loneliness** **Depression** **Social media (fear of missing out)** **Expectations** **Need to live up to expectations** **Regret** **Anger** **Lack of confidence**

Table 4. Academic Stages and Challenges

ATHLETIC IDENTITY AND ENTITLEMENT

Athletes are fueled by the passion to compete, but they are also driven by the entitlement factors associated with their respective sport or simply by being an athlete. Sport related entitlement is the strongest driving force behind the shaping of an athlete's worldview. The amount of rewards, gifts, social media interaction, and accolades given to athletes over a specific time period results in an unconscious superiority or entitlement complex.

For the athlete, this is an exaggerated feeling of one's own superiority. Feelings are exaggerated in that the athlete due to sport related entitlement factors; it magnifies their existence beyond the limits of truth; it overstates their importance or disproportionately exaggerates the circumstance. In many cases, the situation we refer to is playing on the professional level. In other professions, entitlement or superiority may also be displayed; however, the amount of time dedicated to becoming an elite or professional athlete is far greater than other professions.

Politicians, actors, and reality stars have been accused of exhibiting entitled behavior. For example, in the political culture there are many instances where elected officials abuse their power to feed their own selfish needs. However, the sport culture is comprised of individuals who are selected simply based on years of training and practice as well as the athletic ability or potential. Therefore, why is the word entitlement used in a negative way when it pertains to athletes?

The word entitlement is usually cited when athletes exhibit negative behavior or make poor choices. Understanding entitlement starts with accepting the obvious. Athletes are entitled, and that is a fact. However, if you have never dedicated roughly 10 to 20 years, or the majority of your free time, to watching, learning, practicing, traveling, and playing a sport, one could understand why an athlete's sense of entitlement could be difficult to accept. In fact, most athletes do not believe they act entitled. They believe anything given to them was earned because of the years of hard work they put into the sport. According to Megan Pulido, a former collegiate volleyball player at the University of Memphis:

> I don't know of any athletes at my school who think they are entitled to anything. I feel like we have a very strong work ethic in that we need to work for everything that we get and if we do get benefits like the clothes and things we get its because we worked so hard for it.[42]

Scooter Barry, a former collegiate and international basketball player, echoes Pulido's sentiment. According to Barry:

> Most athletes have a warped sense of reality; a combination of the money and the special treatment given to the athlete is the foundation of the problem." He continues, "Athletes know they are being treated differently due to their athletic status, and they become accustomed to it. The people who treat them special, need to realize the damage they are causing.[43]

This perceived warped sense of reality that Barry refers to is actually a common way of life for the athlete. It is far from being warped because being treated differently from their non-athlete counterparts is all these individuals know. If we look at Table 3, we can clearly see how the special treatment given to athletes over time evolves and in many cases increases, establishing a reality or worldview, that is much different than the non-athlete.

It is important to note that benefits athletes receive start during their elementary years and top out in their early thirties. Years filled with privileged treatment usually means a person would have to assume a new identity in order to function in society once sports participation is complete. We can all agree that the move from athlete to former athlete is inevitable; therefore, proper preparation should begin the moment a student athlete becomes serious about sports participation.

The reaction to the benefits associated with athletic ability is similar to a person who tries drugs for the first time and enjoys the reaction; they want more. The more an athlete receives, the more they desire. This is when they began to dedicate themselves to the sport. The beginning stages in elementary and middle school are the points of entry for many engaging in sport culture.

We see the building blocks for athletics as follows: elementary school, middle school, high school, college, and post collegiate ranks such as the professional level either domestically or internationally. However, in many cases we fail to recognize the post athletic stage of an athlete's journey. The post athletic stage can occur at any time for an athlete beginning in middle school. As previously mentioned, the amount of time dedicated to a sport from the beginning stages mirrors no other profession. Time becomes a major contributor to an athlete's entitlement belief.

TIME AS A CONTRIBUTOR TO ATHLETIC IDENTITY

Although athletes encounter a host of entitlement contributors, the number one entitlement contributor is time. Time management can have the largest impact, both positive and negative, for athletes from all levels. According to Kirstin Lundy, an Academic Advisor and Learning Specialist for Penn State University:

> Time management and reading are the biggest issues for freshman athletes. Almost immediately after their arrival on campus, athletes struggle to find the right balance between academics and athletics. They often become overwhelmed with the expectations placed on them, and for some, it takes a while to figure out a time management plan and system that works for them.[44]

Jennifer Abercrumbie, a former student athlete at Temple University and current graduate student, recalls:

> Many of the student athletes I worked with had issues with time management. Throughout high school and their first year or two in a new environment, they were told when to be somewhere, how to get someplace, what clothes to wear, etc.[45]

As an athlete moves up the ladder in athletic ability entitlement, the related contributors grow, thereby making the risk of negative behavior greater if proper nurturing is not interjected into an athlete's development. The ultimate goal for many athletes is to compete at the next or highest level of their sport. While initially time commitment is not a conscious priority for most athletes during elementary and middle school, once they reach high school and college, the entitlement contributors become major factors as it pertains to their worldview.

There are roughly 35 million kids playing organized sports each year between the ages of five to eighteen. Sixty percent of these kids play sports outside of their school.[46] According to the faith community church, 70% of these kids will quit by age thirteen.[47] The process of transitioning into an identity for many of these kids is an area we know little about nor have we explored.

ATHLETIC IDENTITY: ELEMENTARY AND MIDDLE SCHOOL

This component of athletic identity is the start of a pattern of benefits associated with an individual's potential relative to their athletic ability at their age. The structure of a young athlete's daily activities is dependent on their family. This is to be expected; at this level, parents and family primarily manage their time. For example, since this age group is too young to drive, parents and family members share the responsibility of taking athletes to and from athletic related events such as games and practices, purchasing sports apparel, hiring personal skill development trainers, and covering AAU team registration payments. Additionally, parents are responsible for communicating with coaches and teachers via email and text on behalf of athletes regarding practice, game times, and missing assignments of the young athlete.

Parents and family members encourage kids to excel in sports for a variety of reasons. As reported in chapter two, for parents and family members of youth level AAU basketball players, the goals for them and their child for basketball participation were identified as the following:

- Enjoy Sports (16%)
- Get an athletic scholarship (16%)
- Make the high school team (24%)
- All of the above (44%)[48]

With these goals in mind, the dedication to time spent on sports for our youth are largely associated with the possibility of playing on the next level.

Teachers in elementary and middle school are disconnected from the youth level of sport participation. Teachers on this level are mainly concerned about state standards and addressing curriculum targets, particularly in the public school sector. This sector is less concerned about sport related activities and more focused on the academic delivery and behavior of students. On this level we fail to, or refuse to, classify students that participate in sport as student athletes. Athletes in this group are dedicating so much time to sports that their academic foundation is not being developed on par with their non-sport participating peers, beginning in high school.

The number one reason we fail to classify students as student athletes on this level revolves around knowledge of the subject matter and money. Classifying students as student athletes would mean we would have to provide support services for this group of individuals, and these services require a specific program, backed by a revenue source. Most school districts do not have a revenue stream for programs targeting personal development for youth athletes. Therefore, the students who play sports actively during the summer as well as during the school year advance on to the high school level without some of the needed athletic personal development.

Social media is becoming a huge part of student development and will continue to play a major role in how students and athletes use their time. Instagram, Facebook, and other social media outlets dominate the youth athlete in a way parents did not fully understand. Experts say that many athletes use social media for one main reason: fear of missing out (FOMO). FOMO is the reason an athlete's time, particularly at this age group, is spent online and "teched-up." However, as previously mentioned, parents are using the same communication methods to engage with teachers and coaches, enabling kids the opportunity to learn one of the key benefits to using their smart phones.

YouTube has become a way for athletes to showcase their talent and potential skills. This time spent posting and communicating with friends and family online is also an entitlement contributor in a major way. When a thirteen year old kid can have over 200,000 hits on his or her YouTube clip, this gratification and popularity provides that youth with a number of emotions as outlined previously in Table 4.

SUMMARY

As young athletes engross themselves more into the sports culture, the above contributing factors are increasingly associated with the development of a young athlete's worldview. Time spent being catered to by family and friends; time spent in a sport in hopes of moving on to the next level; time neglecting academic development, and time spent involved in social media all have a unique effect on the thoughts, feelings, and behavior, or worldview of the athlete. The worldview for this age group brings a variety of short term and long term problems for the athlete that currently are going unnoticed and more importantly untreated.

ATHLETIC IDENTITY: HIGH SCHOOL

As is the case with the previous stage of elementary and middle school, students that play sports in high school are not classified as student athletes for the same reason previously stated. Parents and family are still heavily involved in assisting the athlete in establishing an athletic worldview. Parents of athletes in this stage are still acting as a communication agent for the student with coaches and teachers. Personal development for the high school athlete is needed throughout the country and local athletics, as well as government officials, are failing to recognize the need for PPD. Gary Darnell, Associate Executive Director of the American Football Coaches Association notes:

> At the high school level during the formative years, that's where PPD really needs to be. But at the high school level you find people who actually fight the developmental needs of young athletes. When budgets are cut, sports and related activities are the first to take a hit.[49]

State education standards, excluding the private sector, are the focus of the high school level. As in the previous stage, personal development of the youth athlete is not a priority. Therefore, it is assumed by all parties that parents and family are providing the necessary development for students that compete in sports. Without question, there are parents that are providing their youth athletes with the developmental needs associated with sport participation, but these parents are in the minority. While the high school teacher may be aware of the students in his or her class that are on the high school sports teams, these teachers are unaware of the dreams and desires of the students. The needed academic attention for these students goes virtually unnoticed.

Outside of the high school sporting experience, many kids participate in travel ball during the off-season. This participation is an excellent opportunity to interject PPD principles and guidelines, but to date this is not happening. Again, this leaves students participating in sports at a huge disadvantage. The amount of time dedicated to sports at this level increases, and time normally dedicated to social activities for students that do not compete in sports is considered to be a significant separating factor.

The social media platform for this group is much larger than the previous younger group, and the time spent online is greater. This is simply because the interest level in sports increases, and the sport-centered social media outlets are in abundance. High school athletic departments are becoming active in the social media market as it pertains to the high school sports program. Most programs have Twitter accounts, Facebook accounts, and access to many other social media outlets. The social media markets have provided many high schools with the same business opportunities that currently benefit college athletic departments. High school athletic departments are now promoting their sports, but more importantly, they are promoting their student athletes.

Television and online streaming has introduced American high school sports to the globe. This coverage has started a surge in the number of high school and travel ball programs. High school and travel ball activities can be streamed, downloaded, uploaded, tweeted and posted worldwide, giving athletes and coaches the illusion that they are larger than life. This is not only promoting a false sense of athletic ability, but also a false sense of popularity, which directly shapes a kid's relationship with athletic identity and specifically his/her worldview.

Another key factor in shaping an athlete's worldview is the entire recruitment process. For football in particular, this includes National Signing Day. The treatment given to athletes during the recruiting phase and visits is the closest thing to being treated like a celebrity. The pressure on young athletes to live up to contributors' expectations can be severe. For example, Kevin Hart was the first football prospect from Fernley, Nevada, to ever receive a D-I football scholarship offer. Well, sort of. He offered it to himself in a high school gym filled with his peers. He chose a Cal hat over an Oregon cap and thanked the students, staff, and most importantly his family. There were cameras and microphones and a victory walk while he waved to the crowd. There's footage and everything. The only problem with this story is that Kevin Hart made the whole thing up. That's right; he lied to the school, his family, and the media.[50]

National Signing Day can be compared to both heaven and hell. It is like heaven if you get an offer, and it is like hell if you do not. Athletes encounter a heavenly sensation if they are lucky to land a scholarship that is combined with a platform to announce it, whether on live television or via social media. The process we are witnessing in today's high school sports is the breeding of a new generation of athletes, lost in the hype of their own egos, and on a deeper voyage into the realm of athletic identity.

SUMMARY

Having already experienced time related factors in the elementary and middle school stage, this group of student athletes has gradually moved deeper into the realm of athletic identity and their worldview is continuing to be shaped. As in the previous stage, there are several factors that have a unique effect on the thoughts, feelings, and behavior of an athlete. These include time spent being catered to by family and friends, time spent in sport in hopes of moving on to the next level, time neglecting academic development, and time spent involved in social media. The worldview for this age group brings a variety of challenges that are often overlooked.

ATHLETIC IDENTITY: COLLEGE

Athletes that are lucky enough to reach this level of sport participation in comparison to the number of youth involved in sports are rare. There are a variety of differences for athletes in this stage, starting with how we classify them. This group, unlike the previous groups including elementary, middle, and high school, are classified as student athletes. Many student athletes in this group will encounter the de-recruitment process. This is a process whereby the coaches and people associated with the athletic department treat athletes much differently than when they originally recruited the athlete. Most athletes, especially freshman recruits, have a belief that they are the number one priority for the team based on how their recruitment visit was structured.

Parents and family are still heavily involved in assisting the athlete in establishing an athletic worldview. However, the stakes and pressure are much higher than in the previous groups. For most athletes at this level, years of training and practice have been dedicated to reaching this point. For others, this level of sports participation brings them one step closer to achieving professional status.

According to a CNN study on reading, it is at this stage that we have recently begun to notice the lack of preparation given to academics in the previous two levels. The CNN report, although utilizing a small sample, is a clear indicator that many of today's collegiate athletes were ill prepared to take on the task of college work.[51] This also means that teachers and parents contributed to athletes' college readiness based on the time dedicated to the sport, and the lack of time dedicated to academic preparation.

 Not surprisingly, teachers and staff play a key role academically for athletes during this phase. According to Jim Livengood, Athletic Director at the University of Nevada at Las Vegas, one of the biggest problems he sees is the athletes' inability to read and more importantly comprehend college material.[52] Assistant Director for student athlete services at the University of Mississippi, Sheila Padget supports Livengood's statement by reporting, "depending on the sport, reading is a big issue."

The problems associated with reading at the college level for athletes could explain why the graduation rate for athletes is low in many of the top performing schools across America, particularly when we look at the graduation statistics of minority athletes. The inability to read once an athlete arrives on a college campus is a strong indication that K-12 teachers either failed to meet state educational standards, or that state standards are not on par with measuring a student's ability to be college ready. This obviously makes educators jobs more difficult at the collegiate level, particularly for athletic academic advisors.

Mary Willingham, a former learning specialist for the University of North Carolina (UNC) Chapel Hill Athletic department from 2003-2010, reported, "A basketball player at the UNC walked in looking for help with his class work; he couldn't read or write, and I kind of panicked. What do you do with that?" Willingham was shocked that he could not read. Then she found out he was not an anomaly. Soon, she would meet a student athlete who could not read multisyllabic words. She had to teach him to sound out Wis-con-sin as kids do in elementary school. Then another student athlete came with this request: "If I could teach him to read well enough so he could read about himself in the news, because that was something really important to him," Willingham said.[53]

According to CNN, student athletes who cannot read well but play in the money making collegiate sports of football and basketball, is not a new phenomenon, and they certainly are not found only at UNC-Chapel Hill. A 2014 CNN investigation found public universities across the country where many students in the basketball and football programs could read only up to an eighth-grade level. The data obtained through open records requests also showed a staggering achievement gap between college athletes and their peers at the same institutions.[54]

As a graduate student at UNC-Greensboro, Willingham researched the reading levels of 183 UNC-Chapel Hill athletes who played football or basketball from 2004 to 2012. She found that 60% read between fourth- and eighth-grade levels. Between 8% and 10% read below a third-grade level. "So what are the classes they are going to take to get a degree here? You cannot come here with a third-, fourth- or fifth-grade education and get a degree here," she told CNN.[55]

According to Billy Hawkins, the associate professor and athlete mentor at the University of Georgia, "They're pushing them (student athletes) through," they're graduating them. UGA is graduating No. 2 in the SEC, so they're able to graduate athletes, but have they learned anything? Are they productive citizens now? That's a thing I worry about. To get a degree is one thing, to be functional with that degree is totally different."

Hawkins who admits that in his 25 years at various universities, he's witnessed some student-athletes fail to meet college reading standards. He added: "It's too much for students reading below a college level. It's basically a farce." Gurney, who looked into the situation at the University of Oklahoma, put it bluntly: "College presidents have put in jeopardy the academic credibility of their universities just so we can have this entertainment industry...The NCAA continually wants to ignore this fact, but they are admitting students who cannot read.[56]

In a graduation rate study specifically reviewing African American student athletes in the revenue generating sports, Harper, Williams, and Blackman found between 2007 and 2010, Black men were 2.8% of full-time, degree-seeking undergraduate students. However, 57.1% of football teams and 64.3% of basketball teams were Black men. The study looked across four cohorts and showed that 50.2% of Black male student athletes graduated within six years. This was compared to 66.9% of student athletes overall, 72.8% of undergraduate students overall, and 55.5% of Black undergraduate men overall. Ninety-six percent of these NCAA Division I colleges and universities graduated Black male student athletes at rates lower than student athletes. Overall, 97.4% of institutions graduated Black male student athletes at rates lower than undergraduate students overall. On no campus were rates exactly comparable for these two comparison groups.[57]

Many of the schools mentioned in Harper, et al., study could blame the previous academic levels, including elementary, middle, and high school for delivering a product, in this case a student athlete, that in many ways is academically faulty.

Unlike the previous academic stages, the collegiate athlete is in a bubble and has no need or desire to engage with the outside world except through social media. Gone are the summers participating in travel ball, the off-season is spent on campus or in the classrooms on campus. Managing time becomes the responsibility of the student athlete. Although time management is difficult due to the lack of time devoted in the previous stages, time management is possible. According to Albert Jennings, a golfer for Ball State University from 2011-2015, "With all of the travel and time spent away from home at tournaments all my life, transitioning to college was not very difficult for me. The biggest thing was getting used to the new routine and responsibilities, but with the right focus, it was definitely manageable."[58]

The amount of time dedicated to a sport at this level has increased during and after the season. Watching film, lifting weights, practicing, and travel time has taken the majority of free time athletes once enjoyed in the previous levels. Family time, in many cases, is shortened or excluded all together except over the phone. According to Jessi Greenberg, a former Volleyball Player for the University of Kentucky from 2009-2013,

"Academically, the college student athlete has to do their own work and don't rely on others, because when you get to the next level (college athletics), it's all up to you. You have to give 100% all the time that you're in school and volleyball."[59]

The college athlete has a dramatic increase in his or her social time. Having the freedom to come and go as one pleases is a big deal for many teenage kids, and for the athlete on a college campus this is no different, especially when people now recognize you in a college community. Often we hear that athletes do not have enough time to study due to the demands place on them because of their sport. However, most athletes still have time and make time to enjoy college social life.

College athletics is a business, and the business is booming. Social media has provided a new outlet for marketing and promoting college sports, as well as the athletes that compete. All college athletic departments have become active in the social media sector of communication, including Twitter, Instagram, Facebook, etc. You name it, and college sports are embracing it. In many cases, the social media markets have provided a new revenue stream for athletic departments, and the driving force behind all social media as it pertains to college athletics is the athlete. Athletic departments are investing time in the monitoring of student athletes online as a precaution to ensure that the brand of the college and athletic department is not threatened. However, the investment needs to shift to the benefits and to the needs that athletes have regarding properly using social media for its intended communication purpose in higher education.

The social media platform for this group is much larger than the previous groups, and the time spent online through smart phones is also greater simply because they have more time during the day as well as a greater interest level in sport. Twitter, Facebook, and the like inflate the level of popularity of the student athlete and give off the illusion that the athlete is more important to the world than they really are. Although student athletes in this stage are using technology to communicate in order to see how many people are interested in their daily activities, they come into college without a clear understanding of the scholarly use of something as simple as an email.

According to Kelly Jordan Diener, the Assistant Athletic Director for Student Services at the University of Wisconsin-Milwaukee, "The lines have become blurry and students on a whole engage in much more social media communications which means it's harder for them to move into scholarly communication such as writing papers, studying, researching as well as communication with professors." Mrs. Diener admits to having to offer a freshman transition class which includes topics on how to communicate through email, as well as teach students how to utilize office hours of professors. Her rationale is that in high school, student athletes really do not need to use these methods of communication with teachers or staff members. "You might have a very small number of high school student athletes that will use these methods of communication with teachers, but the majority just don't."[60]

Social media for the college student athlete in many ways promotes a false sense of athletic ability, but more significantly, a false sense of popularity, which directly shapes the student athlete's relationship with athletic identity and his/her worldview. Kevin DeShazo, the CEO of Fieldhouse Media, agrees, "We [society] have built up this idea that the more followers you have, the more influential you are." He continues, "But most student athletes treat social media like a toy and using social media to communicate with their friends, so it's really nothing valuable."[61]

Television and online streaming has made it easier for alumni and interested parties to watch their alma mater live any place in the world. This expanded viewership, combined with the social media component, gives viewers, fans, and alumni a chance to see student athletes more often and seek to become online friends with them, or to follow an athlete with just a few clicks. The added pressure and popularity for the current generation of athletes makes the pressure, rewards, and notoriety much larger than any previous generation of athletes. Television and streaming opportunities also puts pressure on the athletes in this stage more than ever. The fact that your parents, family, and friends expect to see you play can become frustrating for an athlete who may or may not be in a position of receiving playing time.

Summary

This group of athletes is considered lucky because they have the opportunity to earn a college education while continuing to play a sport they love. Student athletes experience problems directly associated with the way time and time management has been incorporated into their lives during the two previous stages. It is clear that academic achievements have been sacrificed in the process of achieving the dream of playing college sports and possibly professional sports. However, state standards and teachers in the K-12 system seem to have neglected the specific needs of athletes in the developmental years. Student athletes invest time in the area of social media, which in turn has provided them with a higher sense of self-worth. This ultimately affects their athletic identity.

ATHLETIC IDENTITY: PROFESSIONAL

Athletes that have reached this level of sport participation are indeed the fortunate ones. The time invested and years of commitment have paid off, and the goal of becoming a professional has been achieved. Parents and family are still heavily involved in assisting the athlete in establishing an athletic worldview and now the stakes, expectations, and pressure are much higher than the previous groups. An athlete's time at this level is split between the sport and their social time. No longer are these athletes marching to the beat of the college coach or athletic department. The time dedicated to professional sports can vary depending on the profile level of the athlete, endorsements, and the geographic market of the team's location.

Athletes at this point are being financially compensated for their athletic ability, and the dangers of the entitlement contributors are at their peak. This is simply because athletes have had these entitlement contributors around them for so many years that they have become dependent on them. The athletes in this stage have a deep-rooted connection to the athletic identity concept because they have been participating in a sport at each level of sports development and can now call themselves professional athletes. Because athletes have reached this pinnacle, much work is needed in the area of athletic identity. Occupying one's time as a professional, especially during the off-season, can have its setbacks. Since professional athletes have been consumed with their sport for many years, once they become a pro, many spend the majority of the off-season training because that's all they know.

It is at this stage we notice the lack of preparation given to an athlete's personal development through the years of sport participation. In many cases, the journey to the professional ranks did not include PPD programs, nor did the athlete engage in understanding athletic identity. The large number of professional athletes that engage in criminal and selfish acts today is a direct result of the lack of personal development provided to the athlete during their years of sport participation. Time devoted to training, film, practice, and academics have been the focus of development for the athlete, but time was not allocated for the personal development of the athlete during their educational journey.

Think about this: Why do all of the major professional leagues in America have personal development programs for their athletes if they are not needed? Throughout the academic stages, we pass athletes along from one level to the next without providing the necessary PPD curriculum. They expect that once they get drafted, it is the best time to start. How about the millions of athletes who never get drafted but need personal development tools to assist them in adjusting to life when they exit athletic identity? What have we done for them?

An unexpected issue that athletes at this level often face is that many entitlement contributors now figure it is time for the athlete to financially compensate them for their years of loyal service, whether these services were requested or not. A perfect example is the case of Chris Webber, the former University of Michigan player and NBA standout, against Ed Martin, a University of Michigan booster. According to *Sports Illustrated*, Chris Webber was indicted on charges that he lied to a grand jury about his dealings with a University of Michigan booster, Martin, who admits lending the NBA star $280,000 while he was still an amateur. "I didn't lie," Webber told USA Today. "The truth always comes out. What this case is about is a 70-year-old man dressed in hip-hop clothes, who befriended kids and said he loved kids, and I believed him. I didn't know he saw my potential before I saw it. Threats were made. Those threats have come to reality. I believe this is extortion (2002)."[62]

Ed Martin pleaded guilty to conspiracy to launder money. He admitted that he took gambling money, and then combined it with other funds and lent it to several players while they were still amateurs. Martin, 68, said his payments included $280,000 to Webber, $160,000 to Robert Traylor, a former player with the New Orleans Hornets, $105,000 to Maurice Taylor, a former player with the Houston Rockets, and $71,000 to Louis Bullock, a professional basketball player in Europe.[63] The facts in the Webber Martin case may be unclear, however, the fact that Martin gave money to young athletes is a clear indication that he was contributing to the entitlement athletes encounter because they have the potential to tap into the professional ranks after college.

The areas of social media, family, and friends for the professional athlete can bring on unwanted stress, anxiety, and pressure for the athlete. These contributors, who have spent years catering to the athlete, now more than ever desire the athlete to become available to serve the needs of the group. The perceived belief that the athlete is now in a position to financially provide for all is one of the reasons many athletes find themselves in financial ruin at the end of their careers. According to Akbar Gbaja-Biamila, a former NFL player and current NFL studio football analyst:

Two of the more significant stressors at the professional level are dealing with family and acclimation to the social life in general. Everywhere you go, people are trying to figure out how to get something from you and many times your relationships are defined by what you can do for someone. Long gone are the days of splitting the bill now that you are a professional and in turn assumed to be extremely wealthy.[64]

The association Akbar refers to is a family and public perception of the professional athlete, and their athletic identity. The athletic identity perception is fame, money, and a lifestyle different than the norm. This perception is another contributor that feeds into the worldview of the professional athlete. Keeping up with this perception is another reason professional athletes often mismanage their income.

Apart from the previous mentioned stress and anxiety, the professional lifestyle will undoubtedly bring on certain addictions. These addictions, for many athletes, are a way of coping. For others, they are and have always been a part of their journey to the professional ranks. Athletes on the professional level have beaten the odds of becoming a professional athlete. The fact that they beat these odds gives them a sense of invincibility regarding daily life and overall responsibilities. Former NBA player Lawrence Funderburke comments:

Being an athlete on the college and pro level welcomes certain addictions such as sex, women, drugs, gambling, partying, non-stop spending but for me, it was The Lord. Many athletes lack the coping skills needed to deal with the stress away from the game. A major contributor for athlete's risky behavior is their perception that they can always overcome and beat the odds away from the game. This has been engrained in them since their early years as they are trained to overcome the odds, particularly athletes that come from nothing or humble beginnings and end up getting million dollar contracts.[65]

The social media platform has become a way for athletes to remain close to their fans and allow the fans to know what their daily activities consist of. Social media for the athlete has become somewhat of a collector's item for many athletes. There seems to be a correlation between the higher number of followers or friends an athlete has and their popularity in the sporting world. However, most athletes have little to discuss outside of what they are doing in the sports area. Therefore, the only people that equate popularity with followers or friends are the athletes themselves, providing a false sense of importance the athlete believes he/she has.

For many professional athletes, Television allows them the opportunity to showcase their talents, but for some it is a newfound opportunity to become exposed. Getting drafted does not guarantee a starting role or a significant amount of playing time. For example, in the seven months following Anthony Bennett being drafted as the number one pick in the 2013 NBA draft, according to *Sports Illustrated*, he averaged 2.8 points and had the worst Player Efficiency Rating (2.35) among 334 players in the league (2014).[66] Although he did achieve his goal of becoming a professional athlete, it is clear that these stats were not part of the goal or the dream of one day playing in the NBA for Bennett.

Family, friends, and social media followers all watched Mr. Bennett, a standout basketball player at UNLV just twelve months prior to the NBA draft, sitting on the NBA bench. Going from star player to bench warmer is not the ideal situation for any athlete, in any sport, on any level. One can imagine the daily emotional difficulties an athlete can encounter. Depending on the level of personal development, athletes like Mr. Bennett will either have a very hard time coping, or alternatively will be able to manage the situation effectively and see playing in professional sports for what it really is, the ultimate opportunity gained through sport participation.

SUMMARY

The athletes on this level are now at the pinnacle of their quest; they are now professional athletes. The entitlement contributors involved in the life of the professional athlete from previous stages now see their opportunity to cash in on the success of the athlete. The professional athlete is the deep-rooted essence of athletic identity due to the number of years an athlete has gone without the necessary PPD nurturing. The level of stress, addiction, anxiety, and overall disappointment professional athletes can encounter from the moment a professional career begins to the exit stages of their career can no longer go untreated if we expect these athletes to continue to perform at a high level. For career athletes, otherwise known as professional athletes, the easy part is playing the sport. The hard part comes when it is time to become a professional in something other than the game. Many professional athletes find the off-season or time away from sports challenging because competing and training in sports are all they know. Therefore, we witness a number of off-season issues or non-sport related issues for athletes due to the lack of coping skills presented during the formative years of sport participation.

ATHLETIC IDENTITY TRANSITION

At any level of sports participation, the possibility exists for an athlete's career to come to an end. This is known as the exiting of athletic identity through transition. However, the athletic identity exiting stage is different for each of the previous groups discussed. The reason athletic careers end vary from lack of ability to politics, personal problems, lack of opportunity, injury, lack of desire, age, etc. However, the athletic identity entitlement contributors are still a factor, and this is usually when athletes experience the effects of the many years that entitlement contributors have kept them in the dark on every day developmental issues.

Without question, as in the previous levels, time is a major contributor, but the issue of time is a negative contributor. Now more than ever, an athlete's time becomes his or her own. No one is setting the athlete's scheduled activities; no one is telling the athlete where they need to be and for how long. As an athlete, your time is officially yours now and you have to manage all of your affairs with little to no preparation.

In this phase, An athlete may initially still be treated differently than individuals who did not have the ability to participate in sport. This depends on the reason for exiting sport participation. For example, thousands of high school athletes will never play sports at the collegiate level. However, family and friends still see the individual as an athlete and continue to enable or distort the worldview of the athlete.

For the athlete, leaving a sport, for whatever reason, poses short term problems regarding transitioning into life without the competitive sport. The athlete realizes that the dream of becoming a pro athlete is no longer an option. At this point, athletes have the necessary time to focus on academic development and to use their time in a productive manner. This may include focusing on a career, engaging in other recreational activities, and having the opportunity to create a new identity.

TRANSITION FOR THE ELEMENTARY AND MIDDLE SCHOOL ATHLETE

For the elementary and middle school athlete, exiting athletic identity and transitioning into high school without an opportunity to participate in a sport is initially difficult to accept because of the amount of time invested in engaging in the sport in the previous years. Also, the entitlement contributors in many ways continue to encourage sport participation. However, exiting athletic identity when students transition into high school, provides many new opportunities for these athletes. Student clubs and other extra curricula activities provide a chance for these athletes to make new friends and transition effectively. There are also associated problems of engaging with individuals that open the door to drug use, criminal activity, and other negative behavioral problems.

These athletes rarely have anyone to guide them or work with them on developing a new worldview. On the other hand, athletes who have been guided through the possibilities of playing a sport on the next level are more likely to establish friends outside of the sporting environment and find the transition much easier. Over time, these athletes accept the fact that the sport was a youth activity that provided them an opportunity to make friends, travel, and learn the basic fundamentals of teamwork. For athletes in this stage, exiting athletic identity is the easiest in comparison to all the other phases, due to the limited amount of time one invested in sport participation.

TRANSITION FOR THE HIGH SCHOOL ATHLETE

The athlete who completes their high school career with little to no opportunities of playing college sports find the transition more difficult to accept. This is due primarily to the amount of time they invested in the sport over the years, and more importantly, the perceived expectations that family, coaches, and friends placed on them over the duration of their high school career. Unlike the athlete transitioning into high school without an opportunity of playing sports, many of these athletes do not have a student body or an educational institution with activities to engage in unless they continue on to college. This can make the transition more difficult.

The high school athlete who is accepted academically to a four year institution may, in many cases, continue to explore sports participation through intramural sports. They may also attempt to walk on to a team or to offer their services to the athletic department as a team manager. In many ways, these athletes make up a large part of the overall student experience on the college campus. These are the individuals that cheer student athletes on, participate in fraternities/sororities, tailgate at football games, and keep college campus intramural sports thriving. Once these athletes begin to engage in college activities, a new identity begins to develop. This identity includes realizing career goals and meeting new friends. Most importantly, these athletes are able to transition out of high school sports effectively by transferring the skills they learned through their participation in sports to their future success.

A large number of athletes who wish to continue sports participation attend community colleges in hopes of one day landing the opportunity to play sports at the four-year level. For many, community college athletics are a last ditch effort to achieve the ultimate dream of playing collegiate or professional sports. The chance of community college athletes earning a Division I scholarship is possible, but in many cases this is more difficult than a high school athletes chances of earning a D-I scholarship. Three reasons athletes attend community college are: 1) they were not able to gain entry to a four-year institution due to academics, 2) they were not ready athletically, and 3) the schools interested in them were not acceptable to the athlete.

However, exiting from athletic identity for community college students requires a unique approach and a specific plan. Mary Ellen Leicht, the Executive Director of the National Junior College Athletic Association (NJCAA), notes, "There will come a time, and for some that's sooner than later, when sports will no longer play such a big role in their life. At that point, it's essential that plans have been put in place and decisions made that assist with that transition."[67]

TRANSITION FOR THE COLLEGE ATHLETE

The college athlete who completes their collegiate career with little to no chance of playing professional sports is usually aware of this during their junior or senior year. However, a significant number of athletes continue to find themselves in denial regarding their chances of playing on the professional level. We witness this denial primarily in the signature sports of basketball and football. The entitlement contributors that athletes have been subjected to for many years have instilled a belief that opportunity at the professional level is a realistic goal.

Student athletes who accepted the fact that a professional career in sports is unrealistic while in college, or the student athlete who has been nurtured and groomed to focus on academic study and career attainment, have already began the exploration of establishing a new identity. Regardless of the starting point, student athletes are uneducated on the problems associated with exiting from sports. Most collegiate officials believe having a degree, internship experience, and a resume are enough preparation for the exiting student athlete. These components are important but do not address the thoughts, feelings, and behavior, or worldview, of the student athlete regarding sports participation and exiting athletic identity. According to Kelly Jordan Diener:

> The biggest change for me was the amount of time I spent caring for myself physically and the available resources I had at NC State, like having a trainer, the facilities and the time. In college, it was part of what you had to do, but when you're not on a team anymore, your mind set changes because you are not competing.[68]

According to Cynthia Barboza, the former USA and International Volleyball standout:

> Athletic departments focus on academics and athletics, but there is a missing link to what happens when your athletic career is over. Additionally, the same single-minded focus that athletes take on to perfect their craft, handicaps them when they're done playing. They have been so focused on athletics [that]they have not given much focus to career planning.[69]

We must understand that these student athletes have invested years of their free time to sport participation. Now, the perceived expectations that family, coaches, and friends placed on them over the duration of their sport career has ended with a degree, internship experience, and a resume which in many cases was never the goal of sport participation. For the student athlete who finds him/herself without a degree, no internship experience, and no resume, the road ahead is difficult, but not impossible to figure out.

Exiting a sport is the first time many of these student athletes find themselves disassociated with the feeling of being part of a team. These athletes, unlike those transitioning into high school without an opportunity to play sports, do not have the opportunity of interacting with a student body, nor do they have educational activities to engage in. They are now placed in a position where they have to engage with the real world. Many students exiting athletic identity after college, only perceive the real world through sport participation or through social media.

In every sports related interview, "we are coached to say it was about the team and not about the individual. This is basic humility and media training 101; there is no "I" in team. This does not translate into athletes selling themselves at the corporate level at all. The whole point of a job interview is for the athlete to talk about how he or she stands out from the pack of other applicants. It can be really challenging for athletes to switch out of the team-first mentality and market themselves as individuals."[70]

In most cases, exiting student athletes from team sports end up going their separate ways and try to figure out how to adjust to this new un-welcomed identity with very little assistance. They do this because the individuals, or entitlement contributors, associated with the student athlete tend to shy away from discussions associated with moving forward in life without sports. This is true unless the subject of the future is initiated by the exiting student athlete, as this is a topic student athletes have feared their entire athletic career. The entitlement factor crushes athletes when they start working after their sports careers. Barboza notes, "Some athletes feel that sporting achievements hold them a place in the career world, and in many cases it does not."[71] According to Cory Dobbs:

> Letting go of your athletic identity and becoming something else hurts a student athlete. They tend to hit a default button and feel the need to go into coaching; that is what we athletes do we just go into coaching, rather than look at the world at large. Athletic identity can be a help or a hindrance; it's in the athlete, and I think that would bode well for how athletes develop that kind of athletic identity pathway that may be healthier to them.[72]

Exiting athletic identity is one of the most difficult challenges student athletes will face, according to Shari Acho, the Director of Career Education and Advancement for student Athletes at the University of Michigan:

> Athletic Identity is a mental thing. You have to prepare student athletes mentally for what life is going to be like. Athletic identity is like the difference between a kid who is killed in a car accident, and a kid who commits suicide.

The parents of the child killed in the car accident get a reaction from people such as, "Oh my God how awful. Was it a drunk driver? What happened?"...the parents get to talk about it over and over again; they grieve.

On the other hand, for the parents of the child who committed suicide, it is very hard for people to discuss, and the grieving process is longer because we usually have few answers, and nobody wants to talk about it. The same holds true for athletic identity. We have a tendency just to say, okay let's move on [with life], let's get a job, come on get over it, but we have never really asked them are you okay, how does it feel, I know you miss it? It all goes back to the two words, athletic identity. You are stripping a kid in one moment of everything they have been their entire life and there is no grieving process.[73]

Preparing for the transition is something many athletes neglect and ultimately regret. Former Yale swimmer Athena Liao explains:

I should have been more prepared for the transition. I should have looked into internships between my sophomore and junior year. I also should have decided on what I wanted to do between grad school and seeking a job earlier. I should have applied for more jobs my senior year, and I was not as aggressive as I should have been. The summer before my junior year, I just spent it training and doing psychology research on the side, but I really should have done more.[74]

TRANSITION FOR THE PRO ATHLETE

Depending on the length of time spent in the professional ranks and the sport, exiting athletic identity has different effects on different athletes. The main adjustment for the professional athlete is finding who they are now that the sport is no longer a part of their identity. The social adjustment and harsh reality of having to become responsible for daily activities once managed by a team, coach, or agent is completely new for some individuals. Additionally, the sheer reality of all of the time invested in the sport appears to have been a waste of time.

Maria Doelger Anderson, in Matt McCarthy's 2009 memoir *Odd Man Out*, reflects on his baseball career in the minor league. His example shows how painful it can be for a player to realize that his post-baseball career is over, and it shows that exiting athletic identity is emotional. After getting released, he headed for home, and realized that he wasn't the only athlete experiencing major transition.

> When I boarded the plane, I learned that the team had just released another minor-leaguer, and the two of us were seated next to each other on the flight home. He was twenty-five and in the midst of his sixth season with the Angels when the manager had called him into his office earlier in the day. We sat in silence for the first hour of the flight. I stared at the seat in front of me while he ran his fingers through his short brown hair over and over and over.[75]

"I can't believe it," he said to his tray table.
"Me either."
"I put in five good years and then this happens. Comes out of nowhere."
His eyes welled up with tears. I tried to imagine five years of toiling in minor league limbo.
"I know."
"I don't know what the hell I'm gonna do," he murmured.
"Try to get back in the game?"
"I don't know," he said. "I'm twenty-five."
For the life of me I couldn't think of the right words to say.
"I suppose I better," he added, "because I got a wife and kid at home and we need the paychecks."
"Yeah."
"I got no work experience, no education to speak of, I guess I could get a job at Target. But I just don't know." [76]

Scooter Barry reflects on his own preparation for life after sport, "After I finished playing basketball, I had to deal with responsibilities for the first time at 40...the first time I ever saw insurance bills was when I was 40, because as I said, all of that was taken care of."[77]

After becoming injured, Marvel Underwood, a former NFL player stated:

> The post-athletic (PA) adjustment was the hardest thing, but I had my wife with me so she helped me get through it. I had good trainers at Green Bay, but the coaches and

people shied away from me and didn't have too much conversation for me. That's the harsh reality of it; it's a business and if you can't do anything for them, nobody wants to be around you, teammates included. That was a wakeup call for me. Once you step out of the bright lights of the NFL, you lose a lot of friends. People don't want to believe it but its true.[78]

Similarly, Akbar recalls:

When you get cut from a team you have no friends, maybe one guy. Guys won't call you, and then when you call them they tell you they are busy. But they aren't busy; they go to practice, watch film, and go home. Many times I thought, come on man, I mean, I was just with the team so I know what you're doing. But it is a business, and this business determines friendships.[79]

Exiting athletic identity and transitioning for the professional athlete does have career advantages if athletes invested time in building a career or business while they competed as a professional. Cynthia Barboza highlights what can happen if an athlete has not invested the necessary time into building a career or business:

Unfortunately, the longer you continue to play, the more "high risk" you appear as an entry-level hire. Someone coming in after ten years of pro experience and working an entry-level position, while competing against 22 year old non-student athletes, will face some unusual challenges walking into that environment. At 32, your peer group has already moved on to high-level positions within a company, and you're starting from square one. That's a tough pill to swallow, especially if you've always been the best.[80]

For professional athletes, a forced exit of athletic identity is difficult to accept and can lead to denial. One example from Marviel Underwood is:

A guy got cut from the team and just kept coming to practice for like two weeks, and they finally had to escort him off the grounds. Playing in the NFL (pro sports), it's like a fantasy and some people can't see themselves without it. People can go crazy because the lifestyle is so fast; playing football comes easy but outside of football is the hard part. Me being injured slowed me down and made me humble. When I was really excelling, I had money, and I was a different person.[81]

Finally, Barboza summarizes the skills needed to master life outside of sport:

In sports, we learn to master the fundamentals of the game. Unless you master the fundamentals, you won't be a good player for long, and the same holds true in the career world. It's a game of catch up, and the more success you achieve in sport, the more you are penalized (due to length of time out of college combined with no experience) unless you are willing to swallow your pride and start at the bottom and work your way to the top.[82]

SUMMARY

The juxtaposition to an athlete's often hidden vulnerabilities, the paradox of the invincible and the invisible, are displayed as a phenomenon directly linked to the concept of athletic identity in this chapter. The governing bodies in sports as well as the athletic community, particularly on the collegiate level, have allowed the Brewer et al. definition of athletic identity to be the driving force in our understanding with little justification regarding athlete behavior as it pertains to athletic identity. Examining athletic identity for this generation and future generations of student athletes is vital for athletes' long-term success. Our society is consistently evolving and introducing new and exciting ways to study human behavior.

The athlete has been studied for decades in reference to sport performance as opposed to personal development. This neglect in scholarly research explains why the athlete is a mystery to many. The journey that athletes encounter involves a number of complex events, which over time can lead to unlimited success inside and outside of the sporting environment. However, being an athlete includes complex issues, and unless someone has been or is currently an athlete, non-athletes may never understand. Athletic identity is defined as the level of maturity and understanding an athlete has in his/her efforts to maximize opportunities.

ATHLETIC IDENTITY: INVINCIBLE AND INVISIBLE, THE PERSONAL DEVELOPMENT OF THE ATHLETE

The notion of athletic identity brings on a feeling of *invincibility,* which at times can lead to issues that traditionally have been unseen or *invisible.* Our understanding of an athlete's thoughts, feelings, and behavior can provide unique perspectives on the evolution of an athlete's worldview through middle school and beyond. Athletic identity is *invincible* in that athletes cannot escape the effects of athletic participation, and simultaneously *invisible* because helping professionals have failed to recognize or accept that understanding the worldview of the athlete is necessary.

The lack of attention and research in the areas of personal development and athletic identity can explain how entitlement contributors and sport related stages shape an athlete's worldview. Athletes as well as the athletic community face unique challenges in shaping an athlete's worldview. For the athlete, a key area will be on transition and how the preparation and assistance is delivered once an athletic career is complete. The biggest sector challenges are accepting that the need is great, athletic identity is real, and finally that the issues and problems associated with athletic identity are no longer invisible.

CHAPTER FOUR

A MODEL OF ATHLETIC PERSPECTIVES

Similarly, anyone who competes as an athlete does not receive the victor's crown except by competing according to the rules [2 Timothy 2:5]

THE ATHLETE'S WORLDVIEW

In the last chapter, we examined the academic and athletic stages of an athlete's identity, the challenges within sports culture, and the entitlement factors associated with shaping an athlete's worldview. In addition to advancing through chronological stages from elementary school through the professional level, athletes also experience different perspectives throughout their athletic journeys. An athlete's worldview is comprised of five different perspectives: Initial, Invincible, Invisible, In-between, and Independent.

The five perspectives of an athlete's worldview are outlined in figure 3. Unlike the athletic phases, which are based on age and level of sport, these perspectives are in some cases intertwined and are not always permanent because an athlete's worldview is a continuous and evolving approach to entering and exiting the athletic identity construct. An athlete can experience one or several athletic perspectives over the course of a journey through athletics, and in many cases will experience multiple categories at once in the three developmental areas of PPD: personal, social, and professional.

The worldview of the athlete is primarily based on the psyche of the athlete. However, the behavior of an athlete, or their maturity and growth, is the process of actually acting on the psyche developed as a result of sport participation. The five athletic perspectives have a unique and direct connection to the psyche, resulting in the behavior of athletes. A closer look at the behavior will be introduced in the following chapter to provide a thorough understanding of the worldview and athletic perspectives as they relate to the behavior displayed by athletes.

The underlying construct of the worldview of the athlete is quite simple. Athletes think from a perspective based on external sport-related factors. This thinking makes the athlete feel a certain way about their personal, social, and professional development (PSP), which in turn ultimately affects the behavior of the athlete in the PSP development areas. The construct of an athlete's overall worldview, in many ways, provides an explanation of the mystery surrounding the psyche, behavior, and growth (maturity) of the athlete from a number of different athletic perspectives. These perspectives, when understood properly, give athletes and helping professionals a clear understanding of the specific make-up or psyche of athletes participating in sport.

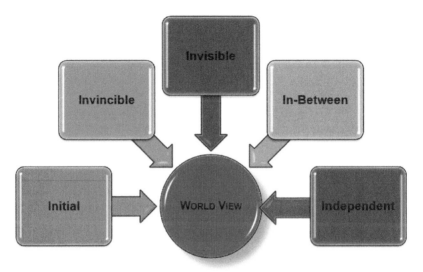

Figure 3. Model of Athletes Perspectives [MAP]

Athletes Worldview Perspective

This overall approach is termed the Model of Athletic Perspectives (MAP), with the various perspectives comprising the model known as *The Five I's*.[83] The MAP approach can be described as a dual theory to help athletes and practitioners understand the athletic worldview, or psyche, as well as the mental and behavioral stages of athletes from entry to exit at all levels of sport. The mental aspects of the theory are the essence of athletic identity because they trigger appropriate and inappropriate behavior. The MAP allow athletes and practitioners the ability to determine a starting point in the helping relationship while pinpointing where growth needs to take place, and more importantly, how development can be measured.

THE FIVE I'S

THE INITIAL PERSPECTIVE

The first perspective of the athlete's worldview is termed the *Initial Perspective*. At this point, the athlete has usually played club sports, youth sports, Amateur Athletic Union (AAU) sports while in high school, and has entered their first year of college. These athletes believe they have a very good chance of competing in professional or Olympic sports once they complete college. The entitlement contributors reinforce this belief as discussed in the previous chapter.

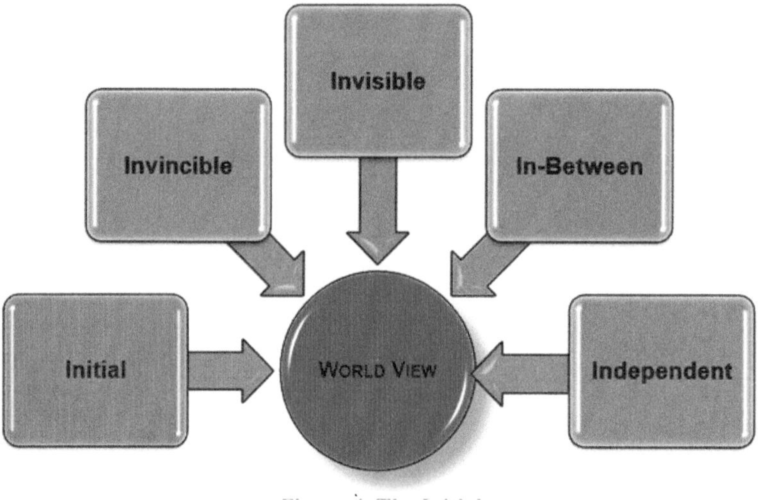

Figure 4. The Initial

The mentality of these athletes relates to the sports they play. This mentality began in elementary school, and in many cases continued on into college. Once in college, these athletes see school as a way of fine-tuning their athletic skills to enable them to play professionally. As far as the athlete is concerned, attending college is only a means to an end. Academics and any non-sport related activities are of no real interest to athletes in this stage, primarily because the main reason they are attending college is based on their athletic ability. The elements that make up the athlete's mindset in the *Initial Perspective* are outlined in figure 5. In this perspective, athletes possess a serious thought process focusing on athletic development, a feeling of personal freedom related to being away from home for the first time, and a cautious approach towards academic and professional development.

Although their academic pursuits assisted these athletes in gaining entry to college, athletics was the number one reason they were recruited. More importantly, athletics is ultimately the reason they will continue to persist on campus. Lack of academic or athletic performance could result in the loss of a scholarship, unless the student is attending college on an academic scholarship. Therefore, the number one priority for college student athletes is maintaining a mental focus on their sport.

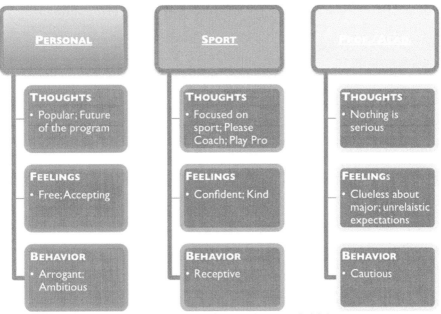

Figure 5. Athletes Mindset Elements, Initial

The student athlete attending college on an academic scholarship can also display a state of mind connected to the *Initial Perspective*. According to Athena Liao, a former student athlete at Yale University in swimming from 2009-2013:

> All of the Yale athletes are smart and work hard in the classroom, [and] although they don't give athletic scholarships, people still complain about being so busy in sport. But at the end of the day, we are really students first, and that's a big difference between scholarship athletes and non-scholarship athletes. Another difference is how the scholarship athlete is tied to the university through sport. If I wanted to quit the team and just continue to go to school, I could have at any time and my decision would not

have affected my status at the institution. This is something that happens with non-scholarship athletes all the time. I guess the pressure is less to perform in some cases, because you know your sports participation is something you can walk away from at any time. People come and go all the time. If someone decided to leave, there's really nothing the coach can do, and you can continue to attend school.[84]

The *Initial Perspective* of the student athlete is compounded by the desire to please the coach or coaches. These student athletes will virtually do anything the coach asks because in their mind the coach or coaching staff is their ticket to the next level. Attending extra film sessions, shooting extra shots, running extra sprints, etc., are all done with one goal in mind: to play as much as possible. In certain situations, athletes will agree to redshirt or not play their first year of college just to stay in good standing with coaches. They will ignore the fact that coaches will still recruit athletes for the following year. This places the redshirt athlete in a position to battle for a starting spot or playing time, reinforcing the fact that nothing is guaranteed.

The *Initial Perspective* of the athlete's worldview can be deemed as genuine and normal for student athletes, particularly competing in signature sports such as football and basketball. Athletes who are lucky enough to have the opportunity to compete in these environments worked hard to get there. Through hard work, they deserve the scholarships offered based on their athletic ability. Student athletes in the *Initial Perspective* are still naive to the realities of sport.

THE INVINCIBLE PERSPECTIVE

The *Invincible Perspective* usually begins in the second or third year of college, and it extends to the professional ranks. Due to the success they had during the first few years of playing college or high school sports, they believe they are undoubtedly going to be able to make a living through playing professional sports. The entitlement contributors have fueled the athletes' mentality and, up until this point in their careers, provided an unrealistic level of confidence regarding their true ability and their potential to play on the professional ranks.

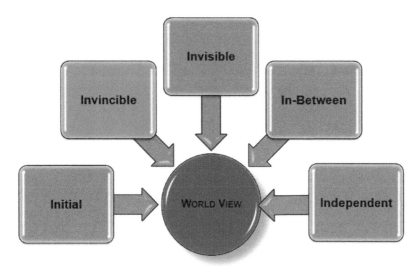

Figure 6. The Invincible

Athletes with-in the *Invincible Perspective* have unique opportunities to take full advantage of their sport participation or status as an athlete. These are athletes that have been on campus for more than one semester and have had the opportunity to engage in outside activities, but have not been encouraged to do so. These athletes view non-sport related opportunities as unimportant in relation to sport related success. Some of the elements that make up the psyche of athletes in the *Invincible Perspective*, as seen in figure 7, contribute to these athletes developing a false perception of how others view them. Athletes in this perspective often express inconsiderate feelings, behave in an "above-the-law" manner, and have little-to-no interest in non-sport related activities.

The athlete experiencing the *Invincible Perspective* view college and university activities and programs that are designed for non-student athletes as opportunities for people who do not have a chance of playing professional sports. In other words, these programs are not for the athlete with an invincible attitude, because they think they are going to become a professional. The main reason for this mental approach is that the only activity that has ever gained these individuals attention and status, whether in their family, on campus, or in their community, is being an athlete. Additionally, if the athlete in the invincible mindset starts to focus on anything other than sport, they believe this shift in focus could possibly ruin their chances of becoming a professional.

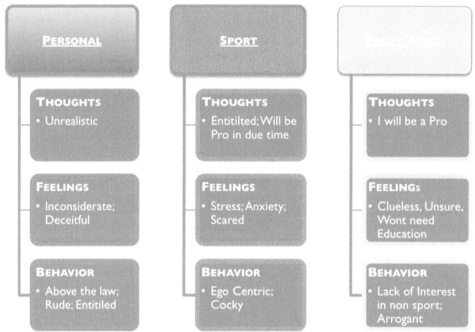

Figure 7. Athletes Mindset Elements Invincible

The mental approach for athletes in this perspective is in many ways focused on a potential opportunity of playing professional sports. More importantly, they are focused on earning a salary that they think would place them in a better position financially. In a study on athletes' perceptions, 64% of the athletes indicated that they would have accepted fifty thousand dollars a year to play a sport and would have forgone attending college simply because they were only attending college as a means to enter into the world of professional sports.[85]

In the *Invincible Perspective*, the majority of personal, social, and professional problems for athletes occur. The amount of stress and anxiety the athlete encounters as a result of years of influence by the entitlement contributors build to this point. For athletes at this stage, becoming all they can be may not be enough to live up to the expectations set by entitlement contributors. Therefore, the athlete with an invincible mentality psychologically projects his or her importance on a level that he or she may never achieve. This in turn creates an unconscious trigger of emotions directly related to the athlete's mentality, specifically, the attitude the athlete has toward themselves and toward other people. The athlete, from this perspective, believes that they can do anything they desire because they are above everyone and anything. This includes the law.

The mentality of the athlete in this stage is an overall direct result of information the athlete has either been told, experienced, or witnessed from the outside world pertaining to sport participation. As reported, 92% of the athletes believed athletes are perceived as gods by society, directly contributing to their invincible mindset.[86]

THE INVISIBLE PERSPECTIVE

The *Invisible Perspective* usually begins in an athlete's last year of college or at any time they realize they are not as competitive as they were in the previous levels of sport participation, or when they find themselves exiting sport participation. Often in this perspective, athletes find themselves outplayed by teammates and realize that they have not attracted professional scouts as they had hoped, or have suffered a career ending injury. These are athletes who have finally realized that playing sports professionally or at the Olympic level will be very difficult, if not impossible. In contrast to a feeling of invincibility, athletes now feel that their athletic identity and future is invisible. During this stage, many athletes look back on their sports careers and wish they had done more or had other opportunities in the sport. Such missed opportunities may have allowed them the chance to continue playing at the next level or achieve personal sport related success.

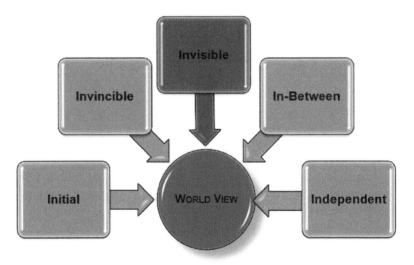

Figure 8. The Invisible

Most often, a sudden exploration of identity, or self-image, begins at this stage. Athletes try to find interests other than sports in which to engage and with which to alternately identify themselves. Also, at this stage, high school and college athletes begin to attempt to concentrate on academic study if they have neglected it in the past, or they may exit the academic challenge altogether.

These are the same athletes who were discussed in the *Initial Perspective*. Finding themselves without the skills that would ensure a professional sports career, they now place blame on the coach, the system the coach used, and/or injury related issues. The athlete's perspective also focuses much of the blame on the entitlement contributors regarding the selection of school or overall lack of sport related development. The elements that make up the athletes' psyche in the *Invisible Perspective* are outlined in figure 9. The thoughts, feelings, and behavior of athletes in this stage include a frustration over the feeling of invisibility, as well as blaming others for their lack of success, a feeling of personal guilt or anger, and a nervous approach towards academic, professional, and identity exploration.

For the professional athlete exiting athletic identity, the *Invisible Perspective* can have devastating effects on family, as well as the individual athlete. According to former NFL running back Eddie George:

> It never got to those depths where I wanted to end my life, but I can certainly understand how some guys get to that point. There wasn't that instant success on the football field, where you worked hard all week and you have a victory and a great game on Sunday. There were some things I had to go through that weren't necessarily helping me and my family out. I can certainly see where guys who don't have the proper guidance or right mindset can take that turn for the worst [killing themselves]. I was fighting demons and trying to get a peace of mind that did damage to me and my family, my wife. Hanging out and chasing (women), and all the wrong things. All the things that served me as a player didn't serve me as a man who's 35, 36, 37 years old trying to redefine himself. Something had to change in me.[87]

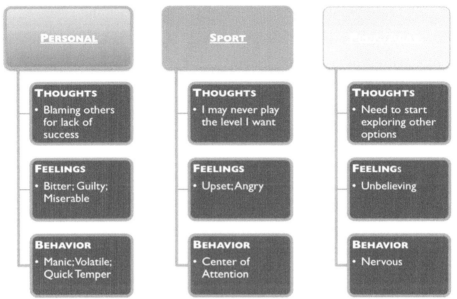

Figure 9. Athletes Mindset Elements, Invisible

The athletes in this perspective, particularly college athletes exiting sport, commonly speak out about the unjust treatment athletes receive in "the system." Athletes, in many cases, insist that they are exploited and blame their university for their own lack of academic success. Although these athletes may be somewhat correct, they do not consider that they are in need of holding themselves accountable. This blame game perspective can stay with athletes for years after exiting from sport, especially if a new and exciting perspective is not identified.

The biggest problem athletes have in this stage is the ability to get the necessary assistance needed to move forward or get on with life outside of sports. Of athletes interviewed, 100% reported that they need a special type of counseling.[88] Eddie George comments, "Some of the things you have to go through to find your next life purpose can be daunting; it can be intimidating, and it can be exciting, but it's a process you have to go through to get there."[89] The process George is referring to requires counseling assistance, or athletes will find the journey to establishing mental peace of mind challenging. George continues:

> What defines success? Is it having millions of dollars, or is it peace of mind? And that is ultimately what I am talking about, having that peace of mind where I am happy and confident in who I am, and what I am doing, and where I am going versus floundering, [and] searching for that

peace of mind. Think of guys like Junior Seau and even Steve (McNair) to some degree, being out of the game for the first time. You search for peace of mind, and you often search in the wrong places.[90]

Donnie Tasser, former wrestler and two-time NCAA qualifier at the University of Pittsburgh, recounts his experience exiting sport and encountering the mental dynamics of the *Invisible Perspective*. He writes:

I started for the rest of the year, but didn't have the success that I wanted. But it was no matter. I had three more years to reach my goals, and I proved that I could overcome adversity. By wrestling through that injury, I proved to myself and my teammates that the team could depend on me. I was ready for big things.

Three years later, as I sat in the locker room at Wells Fargo Arena in Des Moines, Iowa, I had to grapple with the fact that I didn't accomplish any of those big things. I had just lost my second match at the NCAA Tournament, ending my career. There is truly nothing worse than the pain of disappointment – when you work so hard for something, yearn for it with every fiber of your being and then you fail – I didn't know what to do with myself. I was in a slump for days. Every time I thought about wrestling, I cried. Every time one of my coaches tried to talk to me, I cried. It was too much to bear, especially seeing my two friends and fellow senior captains reach All-American status.

In the time since, I have struggled to determine why my career stalled the way it did. I started for four years on a nationally ranked team – we peaked at ninth during my junior season – but I seemed to never progress in a way that some others did. While I hate to blame external forces, I have come to the conclusion that my injuries played a major role. My knee was not completely healthy until my redshirt junior season. Even my redshirt sophomore year I had to endure serious pain; the worst was when I had 120cc of fluid drained from my right knee just hours before a match. The early years are typically when wrestlers make the biggest adjustments from high school. It took me until my senior year to make some of the adjustments that I would have made as a freshman had I not been injured.

But I think the biggest reason I didn't reach my goals existed inside my own head. The time I spent sidelined with injuries had taken its toll on my mental game. They made me less sure of myself, took away the wealth of confidence that I possessed coming out of high school. The killer instinct that had once been my greatest asset was only there half of the time.

While it is hard to call my career a failure – we did in fact win four conference titles while I was in the lineup – sometimes which is exactly how I feel. The pain of never realizing your goals is too much sometimes and it's easy to overlook the good in favor of focusing on the bad. Eventually I will probably come to terms with what kept me on the wrong side of that fine line that separates ordinary from greatness. But it may take years.[91]

The *Invisible Perspective* for athletes is an emotional roller-coaster that can last a few months or even a number of years, depending on the emotional support an athlete seeks out. The athlete in this stage has encountered a sports journey filled with a variety of emotions. It is important to note that not all of the emotions athletes encounter are negative. However, the athlete has been able to function while on this journey for so many years, over a decade in some cases, and they are unaware of the amount of emotions that they have been dealing with on a daily bases. So when the sports-filled journey finally comes to an end, many of these emotions catch up to the athlete placing him in a continuous state of confusion, isolation, and depression. According to Deqwan Mobley, "When I was cut from the NY Jets, I was depressed for a whole year; I did not know what to do with myself. I had been playing football and running track since I was six years old, I didn't even know where to start."[92]

THE IN-BETWEEN PERSPECTIVE

Figure 10. The In-Between

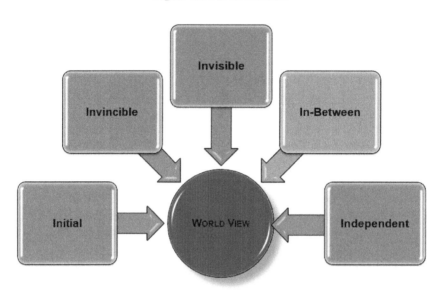

Many athletes will enter the *In-Between Perspective* of athletic identity. Athletes in the in-between mental state can be seen at a number of academic related stages as discussed previously. However, the bulk of athletes with this perspective will fall under the post-collegiate and the post-professional level. We are witnessing an increase in the in-between mentality at the collegiate level due to the little-to-zero tolerance for poor behavior and academic related issues. Some of the elements that make up the athletes' psyche in the *In-Between Perspective,* as seen in figure 11, are frustration with sport and career opportunities, a personal feeling of a loss, erratic behavior towards a professional career, and a volatile behavior from a personal perspective.

On the professional level, athletes who exit the athletic identity phase of their lives ill-prepared for a variety of reasons are stuck with the *In-Between Perspective* because they neglected to imagine an identity other than athletic identity as they knew it. "Oftentimes you don't have a chance to go out riding on a white horse," Eddie George said. "A lot of times the ending, it is written for you, and that happened to me. I didn't have a chance to write my own ending, and that bothered me."[93]

The athletes in this stage are looking for work in or out of sports, playing semi-pro, or professional athletes on short-term contracts playing overseas or recently retired. Additionally, at this stage we witness a number of athletes who are attending community college, leave school looking to transfer, or have been expelled from an institution and have not been able to obtain another scholarship. In this perspective, athletes become the most frustrated and angry. The athlete feels let down by their college coach, friends, family, and agent but most importantly, by themselves.

The entitlement contributors that have played a role in developing a player's perceived athletic identity are no longer a driving force behind the athlete's mentality. In fact, as the athlete's dream of playing professional sports begins to fade, most of these entitlement contributors quickly disappear. Parents, family, friends, social media followers, and the like will continue with their established lives. Many are either not in a position to assist athletes stuck in this mental state, have very little desire to do so, or simply do not understand the issues athletes are experiencing.

Some of the elements that make up the athlete's psyche in the *In-Between Perspective*, as outlined in figure 11, are a pre-occupation about the next move in life, a feeling of powerlessness regarding continuing in their sport, and a careless or erratic approach towards a professional career. According to Eddie George, "The way my career ended had an impact on me the first few years because I had no idea what to do next. It wasn't really until about three to four years ago when I really started to turn around and become more responsible about where I was and not being in this funk, in this depression and so forth."[94]

In this perspective, athletes experience daily mood swings. These mood swings occur when attempting to reclaim the feelings of success and self-worth that competition once gave them; they realize it is no longer available. This mental state can bring on socially destructive behavior, criminal activity, and experimental or increased levels of drug use. The *In-Between Perspective* for many is a defining point in their lives, and the biggest opponent they have faced as a sports competitor. This is when athletes need counseling the most. Eighty percent of athletes interviewed identified sport-related counseling and guidance as the specific type of counseling needed.[95]

The only type of help the athletes have asked for over the duration of their sports career has been related to training to become a better athlete. Although athletes do seek assistance in their academic pursuits, this help is mainly to ensure that they maintain eligible status to compete in sport. This is the first time for many of these athletes that they will need to ask for help in an area other than sports. They need help in the area of life. Yet, athletes at this juncture rarely seek any kind of counseling because the help they require is very difficult to find, and asking for help is seen as a weakness.

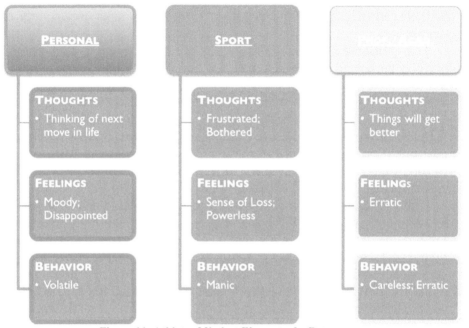

Figure 11. Athletes Mindset Elements, In-Between

Former college athlete Jay Keys' experience is an example of an athlete encountering the mental dynamics of the *In-Between Perspective* when exiting sport. He writes:

> What are my options after that final buzzer sounds? I assumed it would last forever. I was stuck in the facade that everything would take care of itself. Why wouldn't I? That's how it's always been, for me and others like me. It was a rude awakening for me and is so for most athletes the moment you can no longer wear that uniform, and you're stripped of what defines you.
>
> I no longer felt relevant. I didn't realize that the institution I played for had a revolving door. All the years of preparation, hard work and dedication have come to a

world altering halt. There are no phone calls, no try outs, and no opportunity to take it to the elite level. What could I do now? As a kid, I was told to dream and not only dream the dream but chase it. The problem was the odds of me achieving that dream and becoming a pro is less than one in a million. Other than sport, my time on campus was a complete waste. I didn't develop any skills. I never took courses seriously. Hell, at times I didn't even know what I was majoring in. I was just there for what turns out to be all the wrong reasons.

7, 6, 5…

When the question was posed to me, "what do you see yourself doing for the rest of your life?" My mind drew a blank. As a former athlete, I entered the "real world" lost and scrambling to find direction, hoping to feel relevant again. But now the Athletic Identity has faded, the respect is gone, I am a has-been, washed up, no sense of belonging. What team will I play for now? Who will cater to me? No more free meals, no more free shoes and gear, no more handshakes with crisp bills in the palm from a booster. Is this really life?

For a moment yes… I skipped a class here, I miss an assignment there, and yet it all goes away. No consequences and no repercussions. Not realizing that in the long run that what I thought were favors; we dub as "looking out" was nothing more than a set up. A set up for what will ultimately turn out to be your set back when reality sets in.

4, 3, 2…

The details of my dream that came with "the dream" I was not prepared for. How do I overcome the mental trauma of not making it? How do I deal with the pain of people looking at me and treating me different? I was no longer idolized. I am now forced in society to compete broken, unsure, with self-doubt and no direction.

My dilemma is far too common among athletes. So, where's the help, where's the support system to reassure the former athlete that they are elite? Where's the guidance to help the athlete put it all together when his or her mental toughness is broken? The alumni provides no support. No contacts that will put you in position to be successful and financially free.

Athletes are used, and the money they help generate for the institution is greatly appreciated, but in return they offered us the chance at a certificate for "free." Don't misunderstand the point. The certificate is greatly appreciated, but when you're not prepared to utilize the certificate, it's just simply a good looking piece of paper. The paper or degree will not keep you warm at night. Is that truly enough when most of the athletes come from impoverished situations and family members lacking the necessary education and don't value a educations worth. Single parent homes consist of minimal guidance, and we're forced to deal with scenarios that we have not been prepped for. In other words, if we don't see it, don't live it, don't feel, don't touch it, we often don't understand it and when that's the case, we have trouble applying it.

If the institutions truly cared about us as human beings and not just athletes, then there would be an investment to provide services for personal player development. To prepare current athletes for the long-term goal of life and in doing so, the former athlete will continue to have the confidence to be a contributor. Where is the support system to catch them before they get spit out of the revolving door?

1, 0… Times up! You are far from that.
Athletes are designed to be great. Understand that sometimes adversity presents itself stronger for athletes because of the level of greatness within us. My time in the uniform ran out, but the final score has yet to be determined. Life can present itself in spurts and seasons change.

So when you find yourself down, don't panic, because in this game, there is opportunity for a comeback. You're an athlete! You have conditioned yourself for this moment your entire life. Find the inspiration to chase a new dream with clearer vision because with wisdom comes understanding. It's never too late nor too early to prepare to win in this new game. As an athlete, you have the opportunity of rejuvenation by reinventing oneself in the form of what makes you happy if "the dream" is not accomplished. Pursue it, and achieve the level of greatness that is destined for you. You know what it takes to be dedicated and the will to work hard. The table is already set. Remember to bless the food, then eat.

Always, the athlete.
Jay Keys[96]

The *In-Between Perspective* and the previously mentioned *Invisible Perspective* are closely tied together for some athletes. Once an athlete leaves their perceived athletic identity, there will most often be a period of in-between time unless athletes have placed themselves in a position to successfully exit athletic identity.

THE INDEPENDENT PERSPECTIVE

In the *Independent Perspective,* the mentality of athletes will vary according to the amount of guidance they have received. This level consists of athletes ranging from junior high school to the professional ranks. All athletes have the ability to focus on their own independence and achieve long-term goals. Any athlete who desires a scholarship has to envision him/herself going to high school for four years before actually becoming a university freshman. Therefore, in efforts to gain college entry through a scholarship, whether athletic or academic, student athletes have to remain focused for a substantial length of time on both athletic and academic development. These athletes also have the ability to explore and focus on other areas of interest, which many non-student athletes have been able to accomplish.

As discussed previously, exiting athletic identity can occur at any time during the academic or professional level. Therefore, athletes who have a grasp of the *Independent Perspective* usually exit athletic identity better prepared for life after sport. Some of the elements that make up the athletes psyche in this stage are outlined in figure 13. These elements include the athlete trying to maximize the opportunity they have been granted, personal feelings such as feeling lucky or fortunate, and displaying assertive and proactive behavior towards a professional career in and out of sports.

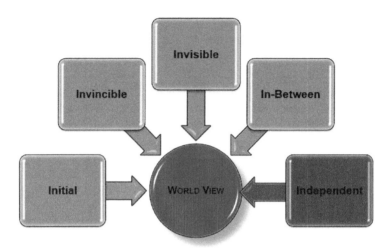

Figure 12. The Independent

Athletes who remain focused on both athletics and academics commonly find varied areas of "outside" interest, even while participating in sports. The degree of their interest and involvement can vary; however, the athletes that actively engage in class discussion and meet with non-athletes for activities outside of sport have experienced a realistic picture of life without athletics. This independent identity, where an athlete is not exclusively defined by sport, makes the overall experience of exiting sport easier. The athlete with the *Independent Perspective* has very little chance of experiencing the negative effects of the *In-Between Perspective*, as it relates to sport. These athletes will experience athletic identity adjustment issues. However, the long-term effects of exiting athletic identity are positive.

The athlete who seeks out an internship during the off-season, and the athlete who ventures into business while playing a sport, are perfect examples of athletes who have an *Independent Perspective*. The athlete who contributes to the development of his sport in his own community by working with young people to provide the same opportunities they once had also describes an athlete with an independent mindset. However, the key visible factor in determining the mentality of the independent athlete is the backbone that defines athletic identity, which is to maximize opportunities they are afforded due to sport participation.

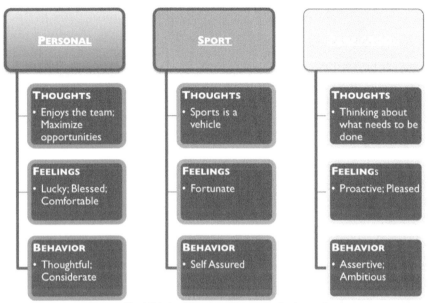

Figure 13. Athletes Mindset Elements, Independent

Jessie Greenberg, a former University of Kentucky Volleyball player who completed three internships while competing, believes athletes can learn a lot by focusing on doing internships:

> I think the biggest thing internships taught me is what I like and what I don't like, but until I actually started doing internships, I didn't know. If you're going to major in a field, you should know if you're going to like working in that field. That's the real benefit of doing an internship.[97]

Greenberg, although a serious student athlete, knew the reality of her athletic identity as well as the opportunities of playing on the next level.

> I have one more season, but I don't plan on trying to play professionally because I am more interested in my professional career. If I attend graduate school I would be interested in beach volleyball, because I have played beach volleyball my whole life.[98]

Albert Jennings, a golfer for Ball State University and CEO of his own clothing company, describes how having an interest outside of sport is rewarding:

It is difficult but not impossible. Not even close. I still go to sleep on most days with the feeling that I could have done more. I've never been one to indulge in some of the things that most college students indulge in. That decision alone gives me enough extra time to create a successful brand. If a peer asks me where I find the time to do all that I do, I ask him how many hours a week he spends just sitting around with friends or partying on the weekend? Most college students would say 10-15 hours a week are spent doing those things. I don't believe there is anything wrong with spending time that way; a lot of people find their fulfillment there. I just use those hours to develop myself and develop my brand. Most of my time on the weekend is spent solely on the brand.[99]

Jennings also believes athletes should focus on building their brand and maximizing their sport-related opportunities.

I believe college athletes have a tremendous opportunity to build their individual brand. For most college athletes, they are at the peak of their profitability and popularity. This is the prime time period to communicate that true, authentic brand of yourself that represents who you are.[100]

For Jennings, building his brand was not intentional.

You could say that it started as a hobby. It was something that I had the ability to do, so I did it, and I enjoyed doing it. But now, I view it completely as my profession. I want to do what I love for my entire life, and I can't imagine myself loving anything more than the job of being the CEO of my company.[101]

Akbar Gbaja-Biamila admits that he always wanted to work in broadcasting. So in 2005, when he was cut from the Oakland Raiders, he started thinking about what he could do until he was picked up by a team. He did not play in the NFL for an entire year, but like most athletes, he had an inflated sense of employability based on his athletic participation.

I interviewed with ESPN during that time and because of my football success, I thought I would interview, and they would be blown away by me. I was thinking, "I am the man," but in reality, all I had was a stat sheet for a resume.

I was told by ESPN I needed to go back and get some film on myself showing my broadcasting skill set. That experience opened my eyes to the false sense of reality, and my attitude as a result of being a football player.

So when I got picked up in 2006, 07 and 08 on teams, I knew I had to use that time to start working on my career or transition plan while I was playing, and not wait until I was finished playing. I attended one of the NFL broadcasting camps, a competitive program the NFL has for players. The problem with the program is they only had 20 spots available. I was lucky and blessed to be accepted.

I knew if I was going to get a break in the broadcasting business, I had to go back to San Diego. Since I played at San Diego State and then played a bit with the Chargers, I figured I could get a shot in that market. A local station, NBC/739 gave me that break. I worked for free, well not free. I worked, and they gave me access to my tape so I could shop it around to the other networks. Then I received an opportunity to work for CBS, broadcasting Conference USA College football. I then moved over to the NBC sports network for a year. Soon after that, I accepted an in studio position in 2012 with the NFL network.[102]

Akbar's story is one in which we can see how he moved through the *Invisible Perspective* to the *In-Between Perspective,* and began to prepare for the *Independent Perspective* of athletic identity. For Akbar, Jennings, Greenberg, and many athletes entering and exiting athletic identity, a host of positive outcomes can and do occur for athletes through the preparation for and realization of end goals. The ultimate end goal is to maximize opportunities through sport participation, regardless of the time in which exiting athletic identity may occur. The athlete who is consciously or unconsciously knowledgeable about the various perspectives of athletic identity, or has received detailed information on the challenges pertaining to athletic identity will, in many cases, end their athletic career ready to exit athletic identity and take on, if they have not already done so, a new and exciting identity.

ATHLETIC IDENTITY AND MULTIPLE PERSPECTIVES

As mentioned earlier, athletes can often experience multiple perspectives of athletic identity simultaneously. Previously, we have not been able to witness the development of athletic identity, and the related perspectives as they pertain to athletes. Social media, blogs, and news outlets have allowed the general public to view details of athletes' worldview, as well as an athlete's mental approach towards their personal, social, and professional psyche. Kobe Bryant, Tiger Woods, Lance Armstrong, and Johnny Manziel have all experienced multiple perspectives of athletic identity during their respected athletic careers.

JOHNNY MANZIEL

College rivals are serious, so when Johnny Manziel, a Texas A&M football player, attended a University of Texas frat party uninvited, it was a clear indication of the athletic identity stage Mr. Manziel was experiencing.

It's no secret that the University of Texas and Texas A&M are bitter rivals. That much was demonstrated in a video of A&M quarterback Johnny Manziel getting tossed out of a fraternity party at UT over the weekend. According to Texas Longhorns blog Burt Orange Nation, the UT frat gently asked the Heisman winner to leave by tossing a beer can in his direction and yelling expletives.[103]

The thought of attending a rival university's social event is an indication that Mr. Manziel was experiencing the *Invincible Perspective,* and the outcome of this poor decision left him in the *Invisible Perspective.* Showing up in the first place was a result of the invincible stage, and getting kicked out was a reality check that he was not as big of a celebrity as he thought he was.

In an interview with Jon Gruden, Mr. Manziel admits, "During the spring, after the Heisman, when things happened so fast, I did too much," Manziel said. "I put too much on my own plate — didn't say no enough and should have said no [more]. I should have stayed in my realm and stayed in College Station and hung out."[104]

LANCE ARMSTRONG

Lance Armstrong became a professional triathlete at the age of 16. Since that time he developed into one of the best professional cyclists of our time, or so we thought. Mr. Armstrong survived advanced testicular cancer that spread to his lungs and brain; then he created a non-profit foundation to benefit cancer research, which raised millions of dollars. He also published a book, *It's Not About the Bike*, about his comeback from cancer. He launched the Livestrong campaign, a fundraiser supported by the sale of millions of yellow bracelets. Sport-specific accomplishments include winning the tour de France for a record of seven times. His sporting accomplishment helped him land endorsements from Nike, Trek bicycles, Giro helmets, 24-Hour Fitness, Anheuser-Busch, Radio Shack, Oakley and a few others.

In 2004, Mr. Armstrong was accused of taking performance-enhancing drugs in a book written by David Walsh and Pierre Ballester. For the next several years, questions would continue to surface regarding Mr. Armstrong's performance enhancement drug use. Finally in 2012, the U.S. Anti-Doping Agency [USADA] charged Armstrong with doping and perpetuating a culture of doping among his teammates. Armstrong filed a lawsuit to try and prevent the USADA from pursuing the case, but a judge ruled in favor of the USADA. In October, the USADA released a 164-page report detailing rampant doping by Armstrong as far back as 1998, and during every single Tour victory from 1999 to 2005.[105] In response, Union Cyclist International banned Armstrong from cycling for life and stripped him of all titles won after August 1998.

Mr. Armstrong's years of denial regarding doping places him in the *Invincible Perspective*. While going through the investigative process, he was in the *In-Between Perspective,* and when the USADA banned him he quickly experienced the *Invisible Perspective*.

In an interview with Oprah, Mr. Armstrong finally came clean, admitted, and put many questions to rest. Oprah gave Mr. Armstrong two examples that describe him: the humanitarian, and the jerk. "I don't know if you pulled those two words out of the air, jerk and humanitarian," he replied. "I would say I was both and now we're certainly seeing more of the jerk part." The interview hit its most revealing at this point, with Armstrong calling his desire to win "ruthless," and he called himself "an arrogant prick," and admitted he was, and probably still is, "deeply flawed." He used to feel victimized by the allegations, he said. But no longer. "Listen, I deserve it. To be honest, Oprah, we sued so many people," he said of filing lawsuits against those he knew were telling the truth. "It's a major flaw, and it's a guy who expected to get whatever he wanted and to control every outcome, and it's inexcusable."[106]

TIGER WOODS

Prior to Thanksgiving of 2009, Tiger Woods was just a famous golfer that most of the world (outside of golf) knew little about. After a regrettable morning, things changed for the most famous golfer in the world. A detailed published timeline by Yahoo Sports clearly displays the athletic perspectives Mr. Woods went through between November 2009 and August 2010. Mr. Woods allegedly had affairs with up to seven women. He lost key endorsements with Gatorade, AT&T, and watchmaker Tag Heuer as a result. He also had fellow golfers negatively discussing his actions publicly. He had cancelled golf tournament appearances. Finally in 2010, his marriage ended in divorce.

Mr. Woods experienced the *Invincible*, *Invisible*, and *In-Between Perspectives* on many levels between 2009 and 2010 in his personal, social, and professional development. For example, losing endorsements is associated with the *Invisible Perspective*. The effects of the ordeal caused Mr. Woods to cancel tournament appearances, putting his golf career in the *In-Between Perspective*. His continued contact with one of his alleged mistresses after the original affair was exposed was a result of the *Invincible Perspective*.

Mr. Woods admitted in a statement on his website, "I have not been true to my values, and the behavior my family deserves. I am not without faults, and I am far short of perfect. I am dealing with my behavior and personal failings behind closed doors with my family.[107] Currently, Mr. Woods is trying to get back on track and maintain his original presence in the *Independent Perspective*.

KOBE BRYANT

In the case of Kobe Bryant, from an early age he was on the path of landing in the *Independent Perspective*. Once Mr. Bryant became a professional basketball player, he became an all-star NBA champion and MVP. Then he got married, had a child and was awarded a generous endorsement deal from Nike. However, that all changed on June 30th, 2003 when Mr. Bryant had an encounter with a woman while in Colorado. According to CNN.com, Mr. Bryant was charged with sexual assault of a 19-year-old woman in a Colorado hotel where she worked. Although Mr. Bryant publicly said he did not sexually assault anyone, he did admit to having committed adultery. The charges of sexual assault were later dropped.[108]

While this disturbing ordeal raced across social media, Mr. Bryant was unquestionably experiencing the mental effects of the *In-Between Perspective* in that his basketball future was uncertain, and the longevity of his marriage was in jeopardy. The *Invisible Perspective* was also experienced by Mr. Bryant during the ordeal because his failure was projected from legal counsel and the media, warning that if convicted, Mr. Bryant was looking at a possibility of serving 20 years to life.[109]

SUMMARY

The overall approach to understanding an athlete's worldview, is termed the Model of Athletic Perspectives (MAP), with the various perspectives comprising the model known as *The Five I's*.[110] The MAP approach is a dual theory to help athletes and practitioners understand the athletic worldview, or psyche, as well as the mental and behavioral stages of athletes from entry to exit at all levels of sport. The five different perspectives: Initial, Invincible, Invisible, In-between, and Independent can be intertwined and are not always permanent because an athlete's worldview is a continuous and evolving approach to entering and exiting the athletic identity construct.

The two perspectives we witness most often are the *Invincible* and the *Independent*. This should not suggest that athletes do not experience the three other perspectives. Rather, these are the two perspectives that social media, blogs, and news outlets tend to emphasize in their coverage of athletes. This media attention exposes the athletes' worldview to the general public, and additionally, highlights athletes' mental approach towards their personal, social, and professional psyche.

In the *Invincible Perspective*, the entitlement contributors have fueled the athletes' mentality and up until this point in their careers, have provided an unrealistic level of confidence regarding their true ability as well as their potential to play on the professional ranks. Additionally, if the athlete in the invincible mindset starts to focus on anything other than sports, athletes believe this shift in focus could possibly ruin their chances of becoming a professional. In the *Invincible Perspective*, the majority of personal, social, and professional problems for athletes (on all levels) occur. For athletes at this stage, becoming all they can be may not be enough to live up to the expectations set by entitlement contributors.

Athletes who hold on to the *Independent Perspective* usually exit athletic identity better prepared for life after sports. These are the athletes who focused on both athletics and academics, and commonly find varied areas of "outside" interest, even while participating in sports. The degree of their interest and involvement can vary; however, the athletes that actively engage in class discussions, meet with non-athletes for activities outside of sports and establish a business presence, have experienced a realistic picture of life without athletics.

The athlete can experience several perspectives at once, and for the professional athlete, potential endorsers should consider investing in a personal development specialist to assist the athletes they endorse. All three athletes discussed previously - Armstrong, Woods, and Bryant were by all accounts well presented, loved by fans and the media, and in large part were role model athletes. In other words, they were experiencing the *Independent Perspective*. The sport related contributors for Mr. Bryant and Mr. Woods were identical: women. For Mr. Armstrong, the sport related contributor that led him to experience the *Invincible Perspective* was a pressure to win, and more importantly, to be the best. All three athletes were endorsed by Nike. The question could and should be posed to Nike: What type of personal development services do your offer to the athletes you endorse?

Nike is just one example of the major businesses endorsing athletes. Although major sporting companies are quick to endorse successful athletes, they are equally quick to cut ties with athletes who display negative behavior as part of the *Invincible Perspective*. A key area of focus for these major companies going forward should be a professional development division for each organization. Through ongoing professional development for athletes, these corporations would be supporting their investments instead of projecting them further into an *Invincible Perspective*, which ultimately leads athletes to a feeling of invisibility.

These athletes, and thousands of athletes across the globe, have and will experience multiple stages of athletic identity throughout their athletic careers. Some of their behavior will be reported publicly while others may not be news worthy for the masses.

Overall, the foundation for these perspectives has been built on the entitlement contributors discussed previously, which most often serve as the lure or driving force, taking the athlete from an *Independent Perspective* to the other perspectives of athletic identity. Until now, an athlete's thoughts, feelings, and behavior have not been described in a way that explain and properly prepare an athlete, parent, helping professional, coach, or agent for some of the challenges athletes will face, along with a map of the athletic identity perspectives which fully describe these difficulties.

CHAPTER FIVE
MATURITY & GROWTH STAGES

Do you not know that in a race all the runners run, but only one gets the prize? Run in such a way as to get the prize [1 Corinthians 9:24]

IDENTITY: MATURITY & GROWTH STAGES

Often in our society, kids as well as adults display immature behavior. However, one instance of immaturity does not mean an individual is completely immature; a particular act or decision an individual may make can be classified as immature. Occasionally we witness individuals who continuously display immature behavior over a period of time, and in some cases, a lifetime. Thus, the maturation and growth stages of the player in the athletic identity journey can be defined as a specific instance or a long-term phase, very similar to the stages of growth from adolescent through adulthood.

The worldview of the athlete, as discussed in the previous chapter, provides us with an understanding of the mental approach athletes have, otherwise known as an athlete's thoughts, feelings, and behavior; as a result of a number of influences over a period of time. The mental approach towards the personal, social, and professional development of the athlete is impacted by specific sport-related stages and influences. However, the mental approach towards behavior is one area that can result in a physical action or actions. Of the three elements that shape an athlete's worldview - thoughts, feelings, and behavior, the mental approach towards *behavior* is the only worldview element that actually results in observable behavioral outcomes based on the athlete's worldview.

The maturation of the behavior of the athlete is an area which requires further examination as well as an explanation regarding how the maturation process relates to the personal, social, and professional (PSP) development of the athlete, under the athletic identity umbrella. Understanding this maturation and growth process will provide athletes and practitioners with the necessary information to explain the physical actions, or behavior, of an athlete's worldview in the athletic identity realm.

THE MONARCH BUTTERFLY

Relative to the number of individuals who start off playing sport at the age of five or six, the number of athletes competing at the high school, collegiate, and professional levels is small, much like the monarch butterfly of the butterfly species. There are approximately 20,000 species of butterflies in the world. However, no butterflies migrate like the monarchs of North America. They travel much farther than all other tropical butterflies, up to three thousand miles. They are the only butterflies to make such a long two-way migration every year. A comparison can be drawn between the long migration of the butterfly and the long journey athletes experience while competing in sports. This example also highlights how athletes differ from non-athletes in much the same way that monarch butterflies differ from non-monarchs.[111]

The maturation and growth process of the athlete is similar to the life cycle of the monarch butterfly. The monarch butterfly life cycle has roughly four transformational stages: the egg, the caterpillar, the chrysalis, and the butterfly. These stages are interdependent on internal and external influences in order to progressively develop and move through the maturation process for the butterfly.

In comparison with the athlete, the egg can be seen as a representation of the introductory phase to athletics at the youth level. Next, the caterpillar is a representation of athlete participation in high school and college sports. Subsequently, the pupae, or chrysalides (cocoon) are where the combination of the PSP developmental, maturation, and growth should take place regarding the sport-related factors and entitlement contributors that ultimately shape an athlete's worldview. If this process for the athlete is delivered in a holistic manner, the final product should result in a professional athlete as defined later in this chapter: a butterfly.

The mental approach towards behavior, as discussed in chapter four, is related to an athlete's ability to maximize the opportunities afforded through sports participation. Therefore, the maturation and growth process as it relates to behavior for an athlete is a transformational process that develops over time. This transformational growth process consists of three general transformational categories regarding growth and maturation for the athlete. *The Starters*, *The Selfish*, and *The Selfless* are the behavioral categories athletes fall into, at one time or another, as a result of their participation in sports. [112] The transformational behavioral stages of athletic identity are outlined in figure 14. As previously mentioned, inappropriate behavior can be displayed on occasion or repeatedly. Immature behavior for the athlete is directly related to the maturation and growth of the athlete during the athletic identity journey. Therefore, immature behavior for the athlete can be witnessed as an isolated incident or a repeated long-term maturation and growth issue.

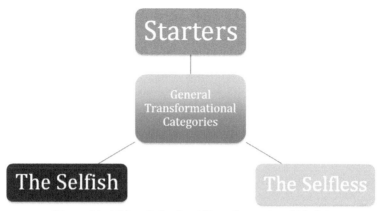

Figure 14. Athlete Behavioral Transformational Model

THE STARTER STAGE

The first transformational stage, termed *The Starters*, is closely linked to Akbar's (1991) first stage of growth.[113] In this stage, athletes can be construed as eggs and eventually will turn into caterpillars. This is when all athletes are simply learning how to play their desired sport, usually in catholic youth organizations, AAU sports, and middle school. Athletes in all sports must first learn some of the fundamentals and how to play the game. During this time, all athletes are appropriately seen as the same because their skills are not yet developed. They lack knowledge about the sport; they are learning and must rely on the coach who is teaching them how to play because they cannot fully develop without an explanation of the sport. As beginners, athletes usually play sports for enjoyment. However, recently, coaches and teams have witnessed a number of young players commonly referred to as "phenoms" who display a very mature level regarding their sports participation at a young age, but these athletes still fall into *The Starter* category.

The level of maturity of the athlete in this stage can vary and is primarily based on the amount of emphasis the athlete and their parents are placing on sports. If a sport is pushed on the youth level, which we are witnessing more and more, there is an increased likelihood of the athlete focusing more on the sport, which has long-term implications for sport-related maturity, academic developmental issues, and a deep association with athletic identity overall. However, if parents and athletes have a unique balance toward sports participation and non-sports activities, the level of growth and maturity regarding sport association will develop and become a constant and productive growth and maturation process for the athlete. This balance will catapult an athlete to the level of maturity of the selfless.

THE SELFISH STAGE: CRIMINAL

The Selfish stage behavior is directly centered on the personal and social developmental areas of athletic identity. The characteristics of *The Selfish* transformational stage can also be linked to those exhibited in one of the personal transformation and growth stages described by Akbar, (i.e., the maleness stage). Instincts, urges, desires, and feelings control the maleness stage. To receive "what they want, when they want it" is the essence of this stage. These athletes act on the mental understanding of behavior in areas of entitlement, criminal activity, self-absorbed, above the law, and arrogance. Athletes displaying this level of maturity can be seen on all levels of sport ranging from middle school to the professional ranks.

The Selfish level of maturity is home to many of our professional athletes simply because these athletes have displayed the same level of maturity as a result of sport participation for many years. The maturity level has not been corrected, and in fact this lack of maturity has, in the athlete's opinion, been the driving force to their success. These athletes see no apparent reason for transforming from one level of maturity to the next. Until certain events occur including loss of playing time, being cut from the team, or exiting athletic identity all together, they will continue to display an unacceptable level of maturity. Athletes with a worldview stemming from the Invincible, Invisible, and In-Between perspectives usually display *The Selfish* stage of maturity.

THE SELFISH STAGE: CRIMINAL
THE HIGH SCHOOL ATHLETE EXAMPLE

An example of this can be seen in the case of high school football player, Jayru Campbell. According to station WXYZ, Campbell was suspended when he punched a Detroit Catholic Central player during a post-game handshake following a loss. [114] One would think the repercussions of this behavior would be enough to assist in the maturing of Campbell. However, months later, sources reported that Campbell, the star high school quarterback from Detroit's Cass Tech was arrested for allegedly body slamming a school security guard. Allegedly, the security guard approached Jayru Campbell in school about a dress code regarding removing his hoodie. The confrontation resulted in the security guard being body slammed by Campbell. Campbell was set to play for Michigan State University in 2015, though he did not yet sign a letter of intent.[115]

Many individuals do not like taking orders or following rules, however, they do not let their mental approach dictate their behavior when confronted with an unwelcome request. For the athlete experiencing this level of maturity, the behavior displayed is normal because of who they think they are. Regardless of being right or wrong, the mental understanding of who they think they are has dictated what type of behavior they can display and possibly get away with.

We are witnessing a growth in the number of high school athletes displaying *The Selfish* level of maturity, as many are finding themselves losing the opportunity of continuing their sport career, and in worst cases, ending up incarcerated. Three Somerville High School junior varsity soccer players were arrested on rape charges after an alleged attack at a team building camp in western Massachusetts. According to CSB:

> The three students were attending Camp Lenox in Otis as part of an annual retreat for Somerville's fall sports teams. Police say on Sunday, the three suspects, who are all juniors at the school, entered a cabin where freshmen students were staying and sexually assaulted three victims. Galileo Mondol, 17, and two other suspects both 16 were arrested on Friday and charged with one count of aggravated rape of a child under 16, two counts of assault with intent to rape a child under 16, one count of indecent assault and battery on a person who has attained 14 years of age, three counts of assault and battery by means of a dangerous weapon and three counts of intimidation of a witness or other person. "These allegations go far beyond hazing. This is rape," Mayor Joseph A. Curtatone said in a news conference. "Our immediate focus after reporting the incident to the appropriate authorities was providing support services to the victims, students, and the families. That remains our focus now," Mayor Curatone said. "In no way are these allegations a reflection on the team, our kids, (or) our community," he said.[116]

The behavior exhibited in both cases for the non-student athlete is a clear cut between right and wrong. Body slamming a school security guard for enforcing the rules, and rape, regardless of the age of the victim is wrong. However, for the athlete, their worldview in many cases allows for this unacceptable behavior.

THE SELFISH STAGE: CRIMINAL
THE APPALACHIAN STATE UNIVERSITY EXAMPLE

The college athlete's selfish maturity level can be considered the epicenter of behavior for many college athletes and athletic departments. When college athletes display unwelcome or immature behavior, most individuals involved in sport misunderstand the rationale behind the behavior. Often times, when an athlete finds himself in trouble and suspended from the team, the university and the athletic department quickly distance themselves from the athlete and provide a typical statement we hear too often.

Depending on the talent level of the athlete, including what they can physically accomplish to help generate revenue and wins for the athletic department, it can in many cases determine the level of unwelcomed behavior that is accepted by the department. In some cases, institutions not only accept unwelcomed behavior, they allow athletes in their athletic departments to adopt a carefree attitude. This leads to the opportunity to repeat unacceptable negative behavior.

In 2012, I interviewed with the Appalachian State University athletic department for the Student-Athlete Leadership and Development Coordinator position. As expected, I researched the athletic department extensively prior to the interview and discovered that ASU had a serious personal player development problem, which interested me due to my education in the field, experience with athletes, and my knowledge of personal development.

During my two-day visit, I experienced a warm welcome reception from the academic staff, particularly Kim Sherrill, the Associate Director of the Learning Assistance Program. However, the actual interview committee did not consist of any coaches from the signature sports, and the only person closely associated with the football program was the strength coach. As I answered questions during the interview, I wondered if the individuals asking the questions, with the exception of Kim Sherrill, knew what they were looking for. Did they know my extensive background with personal development and athletes? Did they understand what personal development for the athlete included? Or was I being interviewed as part of a process and they already had someone picked for the position?

In the end, they hired a candidate who had a Master's of Science in Sport Commerce, and a Bachelor's of Science in General Studies with a concentration in Computer Information Systems. His background did not include the necessary experience to adequately face the issues of the institution, and looking back at the minimum and desired qualifications, the candidate in question did not meet them. To top things off, the individual they hired spent only a few years in the position before taking another similar position at a different institution.

Appalachian State University's athletic department is one of many institutions that continue to accept repeated behavioral problems with their student athletes. As a sophomore, Appalachian State University wide receiver Sean Anthony Price broke longstanding Football Championship Series (FCS) records for receptions and receiving yards, and he was a candidate for the Walter Payton Award as well as all-America and all-conference honors, according to ASU Sports Information.

Price was named National Co-Freshman of the Year by College Sports Journal in 2012 and was the first ASU player since Armanti Edwards to be named Southern Conference Freshman of the Year. Former coach, Jerry Moore, suspended Price during the 2012 season for two games due to a "violation of team rules." He missed the season opener against East Carolina, played the next week against Montana, and then he sat the bench again during the Citadel game. This was a warning for the institution that Mr. Price needed someone to provide personal development in key areas to ensure he developed the necessary level of maturity.

In 2013, Price was suspended from the football team after being arrested on a drunk and disruptive charge, according to police and university reports. Officer Andrew Smith noted that he was stopped in his patrol car near the bar when a bouncer approached asking for help with a person inside. Friends escorted Price from the building as other police arrived on scene. After Smith returned from his vehicle with a trespass warning, Price began yelling and taunting officers, the report states.

The report continues; Price accused the police of intervening only because he was black and screamed profanities and racial slurs, according to police. Sergeant Geoff Hayes asked whether Price wanted him to call associate athletic director Jay Sutton, to which Price replied with more profanity. Police placed Price under arrest because he refused to leave the area peacefully. Upon arriving at the magistrate's office, Price would not exit the patrol car "because no one said 'please.'" At the jail, police said Price continued to be rude and disruptive. "He complained that the jail shoes were bad for his ankles, and he was an athlete. and he deserved better than that."[117]

It is clear by his actions that Mr. Price was experiencing the *Invincible Perspective*, but more importantly, ASU officials could have averted this unfortunate situation had they invested in the personal development of Mr. Price. "I'd like to say I'm sorry to my teammates and coaches, ASU Chancellor Dr. Peacock, and the campus and local communities for the ill-advised decisions that I made that led to my suspension," Price said in the statement. "My actions were ill-advised and immature and don't reflect how I want to represent my team and my school. I hope to have the opportunity to return to the field and represent Appalachian State in a positive way."[118]

The University's response: *"We hold our student-athletes to high standards as representatives of our program, our university and our community," head coach, Scott Satterfield, said. "The decisions Sean made did not meet those standards and, therefore, there are consequences Sean's suspension comes with a number of conditions that have to be met, not the least of which is re-earning the trust of the university, the community and his coaches and teammates. We hope that he will meet these conditions and be able to return to the field at some point in the future."[119]*

What conditions, and what personal development elements would be included in these conditions? These obscure comments indicate that the coach does not understand what Mr. Price needs from a developmental standpoint.

It is clear that the proposed conditions were not effective because according to the Winston Salem Journal, Mr. Price was arrested again two months later on assault charges and other offenses in connection with a disturbance at his Boone apartment complex. Mr. Price was charged with felony assault by strangulation, resisting a public officer, being intoxicated and disruptive, refusing to be handcuffed, and fighting with officers.[120] Again, the personal development needed to prevent Mr. Price's ongoing negative behavior was not provided. If this support were provided, he would have never been arrested after initially being kicked off the team for violating team rules.

The University's response to Mr. Price's actions: *After the incident, Coach Scott Satterfield dismissed Price from the football team.*

In 2013, ASU free safety, Alex Gray, was charged with assault on a female. Additionally, ASU defensive lineman, Ronald Blair, was arrested on charges of "driving after consuming alcohol underage."[121]

The University's response to Alex Gray's arrest: *Gray has been suspended indefinitely from all team activities, head coach Scott Satterfield* *said in a statement. "The charges against Alex are very serious, and the behavior outlined in those charges is not something that we condone or tolerate from the young men in our program," Satterfield said. "At this time, we're going to allow the legal process to run its course. When we learn more from legal authorities as they complete that process, we will determine if any additional discipline is appropriate from the athletics department and the football program."[122]*

The University's response to Ronald Blair's arrest: *"We are aware of and disappointed about the situation involving Ronald Blair," Head Coach Scott Satterfield said in an email from ASU athletic department spokesman Mike Flynn. "We are currently in the process of gathering facts and details. We want to be sure that we have all of the facts surrounding the situation before moving forward with any determination regarding Ronald's playing status."[123]*

As stated previously, the response from university officials when an athlete displays unwelcome behavior is typical. In regards to the arrest of the athletes above, ASU Sports Information Director Mike Flynn said that the arrests were not indicative of a trend of violence and criminal behavior within the football program, noting that the vast majority of student-athletes are "terrific representatives of the university on and off the field." It is always easy to point towards the athletes that are not getting in hot water with the law, but many of the student athletes he is referring to are in the non-signature sports. Flynn continues, "According to ASU head football Coach Satterfield, one incident within our football program is too many, so he, his assistant coaches, and many other members of the athletics department staff work tirelessly to promote positive citizenship among our student-athletes (2013)."[124] Yet in reality, what and how many programs have been implemented since? In 2012, ASU linebacker, John Rizor, was involved in an assault. John Rizor was charged with simple physical assault, according to reports. Mr. Rizor also received a citation for driving with a revoked license according to ASU Police Captain Todd Corley. According to court records, Rizor_was charged with driving while impaired in 2012 in Avery County and is awaiting trial on that charge. Two ASU students, Mr. Cocker and Mr. McKinnon sustained injuries from the assault. Mr. Cocker had an injury in the center of his forehead, while McKinnon was bloody and swollen on the right side of his face, according to the report. A small pool of blood was visible in the middle of the street near Ivy Hall, the report states.[125]

The University's response to John Rizor arrest: *Head coach, Jerry Moore, said in the news release that the player's actions were "not consistent with what we expect from members of our program." Mr. Rizor* *was dismissed from the football team for an unspecified "violation of team rules," according to a news release. "My hope is that this will serve as a learning experience for every player in our program."[126]*

In 2011-12, ASU had two football players accused of raping a female ASU freshman. However, the 24th District Attorney's Office declined criminal prosecution in the case. Yet in a strange twist, the University Conduct Board found the men responsible for student code violations of sex offenses, sexual misconduct, and harassment, and suspended each student from campus for eight semesters.[127] In 2010, Anthony Breeze, an Appalachian State basketball player, was arrested on two felony charges related to controlled substances. Breeze, 22, was charged with possession with intent to sell and deliver Schedule II controlled substance, and with sale and delivery of Schedule II controlled substance.[128]

It must be noted that research on ASU athlete arrests is not extensive and has only been cited to highlight the behavior athletes display as a result of their worldview and lack of personal development as well as to show athletic department reactions. The number of colleges and universities expelling athletes for behavioral issues is on the rise, and rather than injecting a true holistic personal player development program, most universities experiencing behavioral problems with their athletes issue basic blanket statements of what they expect from the athlete. However, as you can see from the ASU example, the institution took the easy way out by either doing nothing for the athlete, hiring someone without the necessary background to build a personal player development program, or simply remove the student athlete from the team altogether.

THE SELFISH STAGE: CRIMINAL
PROFESSIONAL ATHLETE NBA AND NFL EXAMPLE

Athletes at the professional level exhibit an extension of the behavior we witness at the collegiate level. In many cases, athletes that display inappropriate behavior as professionals are repeat offenders of this type of behavior. The assistance provided to the professional athlete experiencing selfish criminal behavior can vary. However, professional teams obviously differ from the collegiate ranks in that the professional teams invest millions of dollars in athletes. Despite money spent on athletes, the professional level does not have an understanding of athletic identity that can assist and explain professional unwelcome athlete behavior.

An example of a professional athlete displaying *The Selfish* behavior is former Redskins tight end Fred Davis. In 2011, Davis failed multiple tests for marijuana use and was suspended for the final four games of that season. He claimed afterward that he had learned his lesson and vowed to mature. However, in 2014 the NFL suspended Davis indefinitely for violating the league's substance abuse policy. Just one day after the NFL suspended him indefinitely, Davis was arrested in Fairfax County and charged with driving under the influence, a Fairfax County Police Department spokesperson confirmed.[129]

Another example: Minnesota Vikings linebacker, Erin Henderson, was arrested on suspicion of drunken driving for the second time in a little more than a month. He was booked on four charges, including second-degree drunken driving for refusing an alcohol test. According to the police report, Henderson also had a small amount of marijuana and drug paraphernalia with him. Another Vikings player, receiver Jerome Simpson, avoided jail time after pleading guilty to careless driving and third-degree DWI. Simpson was ordered to do 120 hours of community service in public schools instead of serving 15 days in the workhouse.[130]

Over the years, the NBA has had a number of current and former players displaying selfish criminal behavior, and in reviewing programs offered it seems as if athletic identity is not a topic being addressed. An example is seen in the case of Michael Beasley who was the number two pick in 2008, drafted by the Miami Heat after earning Big 12 Player of the Year honors during his one season at Kansas State. Before playing his first game for the Heat, Beasley was fined $50,000 for his role in a marijuana-related incident at the Rookie Transition Program. He spent time in a substance abuse treatment center in 2009 before the Heat traded him to the Timberwolves after just two seasons.[131] Any team taking a chance, or more positively seen as making an investment, in Mr. Beasley should have had the proper mandatory personal development system in place to assist Mr. Beasley upon entry back into the NBA. It is not as if the NBA and league officials did not know Mr. Beasley needed personal development.

According to Doug Pensinger, upon acquiring Beasley, then Timberwolves president David Kahn called him "a very young and immature kid who smoked too much marijuana" before he arrived in Minnesota. Beasley was later pulled over for speeding and cited for marijuana possession by Minnesota police during the 2011 lockout. He also shoved a fan in the face during a lockout exhibition game in New York and sued his former AAU coach, alleging that he had received improper benefits during his one season at Kansas State.[132]

Mark Stein of espn.com reported the Phoenix Suns had reached a verbal commitment with free-agent forward Michael Beasley on a three-year deal worth $18 million, according to sources familiar with the deal. The article admitted Beasley has been dogged by bouts of immaturity throughout his four-year career, but the Suns are not scared off by his reputation and instead are fond of him as a player and a person, sources told ESPN Magazine's Chris Broussard.[133] After signing with the Suns, Mr. Beasley himself reported that he was a changed man regarding his marijuana use. According to Ben Golliver of nbasi.com, "I realize 10 minutes of feeling good is not really worth putting my life, and my career, and my legacy in jeopardy," Beasley said, according to the Associated Press. "I'm confident to say that part of my career, that part of my life, is over and won't be coming back."[134]

Months later, after Mr. Beasley received a three-year, $18 million deal, the Suns released him soon after his arrest in Scottsdale, Arizona, for suspicion of marijuana possession, citing "personal and professional conduct standards."[135] The reasons the Suns gave for the release of Mr. Beasley were discussed in previous chapters; two of the three key development areas of personal player development: personal and professional.

The 2013 arrest was the third time during Beasley's tenure in Phoenix that he has found himself in hot water. In May, it was reported that Beasley was under investigation for an alleged sexual assault. Beasley has not been charged but the case is still open, according to the *Arizona Republic*. Subsequently, news broke that Beasley was cited for multiple driving violations. He was cited for driving 71 mph in a 45-mph zone at 1:10 a.m. in a Mercedes that did not have a license plate. Beasley was driving on a suspended license, and a loaded gun was found in the vehicle. Suns management did not discipline Beasley after the incident.[136] This continued behavior places Mr. Beasley in the *Invincible Perspective* as well as in *The Selfish* behavioral state.

Mr. Beasley received another opportunity to continue his NBA career. In 2013, the Miami Heat, the team that originally drafted him, invited Beasley to a training camp on a non-guaranteed, veterans minimum contract, and eventually they signed him. According to Heat President Pat Riley, "Michael had the best years of his career with us," "We feel that he can help." Let's hope the Heat and Pat Riley can get Mr. Beasley to reach his full potential.[137]

The maturity and behavior displayed by athletes in this stage of growth is directly related to the mentality the athletes have ingrained in themselves over a period of time. Often these types of athletes do not realize their behavior is unacceptable until their ability to continue playing sports is seriously jeopardized or complete. The problems associated with athletic unwelcomed behavior need to be addressed prior to granting a scholarship or drafting an athlete, and programs need to be provided for athletes while they are participating in sports. Colleges, universities, and professional teams either do not know or care about athletic identity as described. Many of these institutions are not fully aware of how to address the behavioral issues athletes display, or to employ people who are trained to deal with the behavior of the athlete.

The Selfish Stage: Academic

The Selfish Stage is centered on the behavior regarding athletes' professional development. Professional development under the athletic identity umbrella consists of a professional career in sports, as well as a career in the professional workforce. Athletes displaying *The Selfish* behavior in most cases are fueled by their individual expectations. When an athlete's individual expectations are in jeopardy or not met, athletes tend to behave in an unacceptable manner. University officials' reaction to this type of selfish behavior is similar to their reaction for *The Selfish Stage: Criminal* behavior. They issue a standard press statement, and then they move on to the next recruiting class.

The characteristics of *The Selfish* academic behavioral stage can also be linked to those exhibited in one of the personal transformation and growth stages described by Akbar (i.e. the boyhood stage). The need to manipulate results is game playing or deception. This "boy" as he becomes older, sees himself as a player or playboy, and will constantly try to "get over" on someone, or take the easy way out, while trying to look like he's working hard.[138] These athletes lack interest in non-sport related activities and generally display a careless approach towards academics, and a nervous approach or reaction towards professional development.

Most *Selfish Stage* athletes major in unmarketable degrees but expect everyone to think that because they are attending college, they are doing a lot of work. In reality, the workload may have been comparatively easy because they have been given a college course load designed to keep them eligible, not to ensure they are marketable. Athletes displaying this level of maturity can be seen on all levels of sports ranging from middle school to the professional ranks. However, the bulk of athletes that exhibit this behavior are in high school and college. Athletes in this transformation stage hail from the Invincible, Invisible, and In-Between athletic perspectives.

The Selfish academic behavior is displayed for a variety of reasons. Some of the obvious behavior is a result of athletes who realize that they will not play sports on a professional level. It may also result from the coach's lack of interest or attention, their own lack of interest in their sport, an injury, or a realization that, although they were good enough to play sports earlier in their careers, they do not have what it takes to become a great college player or a professional.

THE SELFISH STAGE: ACADEMIC COLLEGE ATHLETE EXAMPLE

An example of this behavior is seen in the case of the University of Southern California (USC) reserve shooting guard Greg Allen, who was ruled academically ineligible by USC in 2013. Mr. Allen was recruited from Navarro College to be an outside shooter for the Trojans where he shot nearly forty percent from deep for Navarro. However, Mr. Allen struggled to make the transition from junior college to Division I. He shot only twenty-nine percent on three-pointers in the 2012-2013 season and was just two for seven this year. Mr. Allen had played sparingly in the 2013-14 season after being a prime contributor the previous year. With USC having significantly more depth in 2014, Mr. Allen fell out of Coach Kevin O'Neill's regular rotation less than two weeks into the 2013-14 season. Mr. Allen averaged ten minutes a game for the first four contests of the 2013-14 season, but had seen only fourteen minutes of action since the first several games. As a senior, Mr. Allen's career was effectively over as a Trojan.[139]

Mr. Allen traveled a difficult journey from the community college level to make it to an elite level of college athletics. The overall numbers of athletes transferring from a community college to a school such as USC is relatively small. However, it appeared the problems for Mr. Allen began when he realized his opportunity to be a top tier college athlete was lost. Realizing his sport-related expectations were not going to be achieved, he stopped putting forth the effort in the classroom.

The University's Response: *USC shooting guard Greg Allen has been ruled ineligible due to academics, according to a school spokesperson.*

In another example, Mr. Willie Haulstead from Florida State was ruled academically ineligible. A senior at the time, Mr. Haulstead caught 42 passes in his college career, including 38 receptions for 587 yards and six touchdowns in 2010. Yet he missed 2011 with post-concussion symptoms and had just three catches last season. Mr. Haulstead's injury in 2011 can be associated with his lackluster approach towards his academic development.[140]

The University's Response*: Head coach Jimbo Fisher announced that backup receiver Willie Haulstead had been declared academically ineligible and is no longer on the team.*

Three Texas Longhorns football players were academically ineligible for the 2013 Alamo Bowl. Redshirt freshman running back Jalen Overstreet, sophomore offensive tackle Kennedy Estelle, and all-purpose threat, Daje Johnson. According to the team, the three players would not be making the trip to San Antonio for the game. Mr. Johnson, a sophomore at the time out of Pflugerville, started six games for the Longhorns in 2013. However, Mr. Johnson missed two games during the regular season due to an ankle injury. He was also suspended for the Thanksgiving game against the Texas Tech Red Raiders, a game the Longhorns won for an unspecified violation of team rules. Clearly, Mr. Johnson had a lot going in his favor athletically at the time he became academically ineligible. However, the injury and the suspension opened the door of reality that his services were not the driving force behind the Texas Longhorns' football program, and that fact plays in the outcome of one's behavioral approach toward academics.[141]

The University's Response*: The Longhorns announced that the wide receiver/running back/return man is one of three players who have been declared academically ineligible and will not play in UT's Alamo Bowl game against Oregon.*

Finally, we can examine the unique case of Demetrius Walker. Mr. Walker played for Arizona State in the 2009-10 season, where he averaged four points a game. His transfer seemed to be due to the failed expectations of both parties, both individual and institutional. According to NBC Sports, when Walker fell out of Herb Sendek's rotation as the 09-10 season progressed, Walker said he felt he had to look elsewhere. "No hard feelings at all," said Walker, who averaged four points in twenty-three games. Like many college athletes, Walker didn't meet expectations. "I understand Coach Sendek had to do what he had to do. I didn't perform at the level he expected of me."[142]

He then transferred to New Mexico. His reason for picking New Mexico over several other schools is that it is a great basketball town and Walker stated that he envisions himself as a "scoring point guard" at basketball's next level. Therefore, Walker aimed to improve his ball handling and get his jump shot to the point where "teams can't afford to leave me open." The next level for Walker is the NBA and basketball preparation is needed to fulfill his individual expectations. Mr. Walker averaged 7.4 points a game for the 2011-12 season and five points for the 2012-13 season. Mr. Walker was suspended from New Mexico by then

Coach Steve Alford, prior to the start of the Mountain West conference tournament. This led to Mr. Walker transferring to Grand Canyon. Similar to most athletes in this stage, expectations are a driving force behind *The Selfish Stage* academic behavior. These athletes expect to get what they want when they want it, and if their expectations are not met, the results usually end in a host of unwelcome behaviors.[143]

New Mexico's Response: *It was announced that Walker had been suspended indefinitely for a violation of team rules.*

When Mr. Walker transferred to Grand Canyon University, the reactions from the university were positive and pleasant, "We are excited to have a player of Demetrius' ability that has played at both New Mexico and Arizona State," said Majerle. "It is good to have him here at GCU, as he brings with him a lot of experience and can score the basketball. He will be big for our team next season having a guy that we can go to." Mr. Walker averaged 16.9 points a game for Grand Canyon but during the season was dismissed from Grand Canyon's basketball team.[144]

Grand Canyon University's Response: *A "violation of team rules," head coach Dan Majerle announced. Coach Majerle wouldn't go into details for the dismissal, leaving it at: "It's very disappointing for everyone involved, but our program remains committed to performing to the best of our ability."*[145]

What makes Mr. Walker's story so interesting is that he did graduate from New Mexico, and that he was projected to be a college superstar from the time he was nine years old. The points per game could explain where the collegiate problems for Mr. Walker began. A projected all star player from the age of nine averaging under ten points a game his first three years of collegiate competition, seemed to affect Mr. Walker's overall attitude towards coaching and discipline. His academic development or expectations of obtaining a college degree were achieved, but I doubt he would agree that his individual collegiate basketball expectations were met.

THE SELFISH STAGE: FINANCIAL
PROFESSIONAL ATHLETE EXAMPLE

The professional athlete behavior in this stage of maturation is directly related to spending behavior. The trigger for these athletes is to have what they want when they want it. When athletes have millions of dollars, they can have pretty much anything, at least while making money. Each year we see a list of athletes labeled as broke, and the list continues to be updated each year with new victims of immature spending.

In 2012, millions of viewers, watched Director Billy Corben's documentary entitled "Broke." The film focused on the spending behavior of professional athletes who spent all of their money. According to Corben, "The way 'Broke' is structured, it's not about people, per se, but the problem, told by the people who experience it. It's essentially a step-by-step guide, How to Lose Millions of Dollars without Breaking a Sweat."[146] A documentary on how to spend all of your money is not the answer to addressing the problem. Overall, this episode of 30 for 30 was delivered for entertainment purposes, and did not realistically address the personal development needed for athletes.

The documentary excluded any concrete rational explanation or facts on why athletes spend all of their money. Instead, the director included interviews from club goers, bloggers, and the like. Many of the athletes that were broke declined being interviewed for the documentary. This decline was most likely predicated on the fact that many athletes do not understand their own behavior under the athletic identity umbrella, and thus cannot articulate the rationale behind their actions. According to Sports Illustrated, seventy percent of NFL players will be broke two to four years after retiring, and sixty percent of NBA players after five years.[147] These staggering statistics show that the issue of understanding athletic identity as it relates to behavior for the professional athlete is essential.

According to celebritynetworth.com the following is a list of the 20 Most Shocking Broke Athletes, as well as a list of athletes who have filed for bankruptcy:[148]

#1: Mike Tyson – Tyson earned more than $30 million per fight and somehow squandered a $300 million peak fortune before declaring bankruptcy in 2003.

#2: Evander Holyfield – After earning $250 million as a heavyweight champion, in 2008 a bank foreclosed on Evander's $10 million, 54,000 square foot, 109 bedroom Atlanta mansion.

#3: Allen Iverson – In February of 2012, Iverson told a Georgia judge that he was flat broke and could not pay an $860k jewelry debt. Iverson earned $154 million in salary and $30-50 million in endorsements during his career. Iverson was known to travel with a 50 person entourage, blew millions of dollars gambling, lavished friends with expensive gifts and had massive monthly child support obligations.

#4: Michael Vick – After declaring bankruptcy in 2008, over the last four years Vick has spent 95% of his income, roughly $30 million on taxes, creditors, lawyers, and accountants. He currently is worth $1.5

million but in 2011, Vick signed a six year $100 million contract with $40 million guaranteed.

#5: Antoine Walker – Despite earning a $108 million salary while playing in the NBA, Antoine Walker had to declare bankruptcy in 2010, listing assets of $5 million and debts of $13 million thanks to bad real estate investments and gambling debts.

#6: Latrell Sprewell – Despite earning nearly $100 million during his NBA career, Latrell Sprewell eventually went broke. Sprewell once famously rejected a $21 million contract saying he "had a family to feed." He must have a really big family.

#7: Curt Schilling – In May 2012, Schilling announced that he had lost his entire $50 million baseball fortune on a failed video game company.

#8: Kenny Anderson – Despite earning $63 million in salary, Kenny Anderson was broke the day he left the NBA. After filing bankruptcy, Anderson became a K-12 school teacher.

#9: Lenny Dykstra – Dykstra turned a chain of car washes into an empire that eventually included a luxury airline, Wayne Gretsky's $17 million mansion, and a $60 million personal fortune. Dykstra filed chapter 11 bankruptcy in 2008, listing over $30 million in debts to various banks and law firms. He is currently serving a three year sentence for grand theft auto.

#10: Lawrence Taylor – LT's retirement has been difficult to say the least. Statutory rape allegations, cocaine addiction, bad investments and tax evasion have left the superstar linebacker broke today after earning more than $50 million in the NFL.

#12: John Daly – Daly admitted recently that he has lost $50 million gambling during his career. He was also divorced four times leaving him with huge monthly bills and little to no monthly income.

#13: Dennis Rodman – Rodman has not declared bankruptcy, but he owes over $1 million in child support and other debts despite earning $26 million in his career.

#14: Deuce McAllister – After earning millions in the NFL, McAllister's Nissan dealership in Mississippi went bankrupt in 2009, leaving Deuce broke and liable for hundreds of thousands in debt.

#15: Terrell Owens – In 2012, Terrell Owens announced he was broke and without any monthly income. Meanwhile, he is paying $120,000 a month in child support and mortgages to four different baby mamas.

#16: Warren Sapp – In April 2012, Sapp filed for bankruptcy, claiming assets worth $6.5 million and debts of $7 million. The $7 million is owed to the IRS, child support to four different women, and medical bills.

#17: Sheryl Swoopes – The first big WNBA star filed for bankruptcy in 2004, listing over $1 million in debt.

#18: Marion Jones – The disgraced Olympian was left millions of dollars in debt and without a way to earn income after her steroid scandal.

#19: Travis Henry – Henry couldn't keep up with his massive child support payments after he fathered 11 children with 10 women. He was eventually arrested for cocaine trafficking.

#20: Mark Brunell – After retiring, Brunell invested in real estate and bought 11 Whataburger franchises. Unfortunately in 2010, he declared bankruptcy owing $20 million in commercial real estate loans.

#21: Scott Eyre – Despite earning more than $17 million in his playing career, the former MLB pitcher lost his entire fortune as part of the Stanford Financial fraud case.

#22: Vince Young – After earning $45 million in salary and endorsements, Vince Young is the most recent pro-athlete to go broke.

Wally Backman	Charlie Batch	Bruse Berenyi	Riddick Bowe
Randy Brown	Bill Buckner	Jason Caffey	Dale Carter
Jack Clark	Raymond Clayborn	Derrick Coleman	Dermontti Dawson
Jim Dooley	Luther Elliss	Eddie Edwards	Chris Eubank
Rollie Fingers	Steffi Graf	Archie Griffin	Tony Gwynn
Dorothy Hamill	Scott Harrison	Steve Howe	Harmon Killebrew
Bernie Kosar	Terry Long	Rick Mahorn	Harvey Martin
Darren McCarthy	Denny McLain	Craig Morton	Greg Nettles
Jonny Neumann	Gaylord Perry	John Arse Riise	Andre Rison
Rumeal Robinson	Manny Sanguillen	Billy Sims	Leon Spinks
Roscoe Tanner	Duane Thomas	Bryan Trottier	Johnny Unitas
Ray Williams	Rick Wis	Danny White	(TBA)

The chart above displays athletes have also declared bankruptcy

THE SELFLESS STAGE

The Selfless Stage is divided into two groups, the *Junior Professional* and the *Professional*. The displayed behavior of both the *Junior Professional* and *Professional* are often overshadowed by the behavior displayed in *The Selfish Stages*. These athletes have been able to find appreciation of their sport participation and more importantly, have been able to maximize the opportunities presented to them.

The Selfless Stage: Junior Professional

The athletes that fall into this stage range from the youth level through the collegiate ranks. Athletes that are in this transformation stage have been groomed from a young age to become a professional sports person, career professional, or both. These athletes have had the luxuries of being surrounded by, or interacting with, knowledgeable individuals from their family or the sporting community and have a solid base of personal development.

Through their interactions during the academic stages and sport-related entitlement stage, these athletes understood and respected the statistics regarding the chances of playing professional sports. Athletes with this level of maturity also understand the importance of majoring in marketable subjects as well as career investigation. Although the final outcome for these athletes is not known, they are still maturing towards becoming a professional in sports or their chosen career field. Their personal development foundation will keep them on track to continue exhibiting role model behavior on a road to overall success.

Junior Professional Athlete Example

Clear examples of Junior Professionals are student athletes such as Jessie Greenburg at the University of Kentucky, Albert Jennings from Ball State University, and Kevin Green from the University of Southern California, introduced in previous chapters. These collegiate athletes all competed in different sports, are different in gender, and have different backgrounds, but were all introduced early in life to the personal player development components needed to maintain a high academic standard, superior work ethic, and increased behavioral maturation. All of the above athletes behaved in a thoughtful, considerate manner, and were self-assured of their role in sports. The approach they took towards academics was assertive and ambitious. This is how they approach their sport. These athletes, like many across the country, can be considered the definition of a model NCAA student athlete. These student athletes have been able to reach a level of maturity and understanding of sport participation, and they have successfully maximized their unique opportunities.

THE SELFLESS STAGE: PROFESSIONAL

The professional category is made up of athletes or former athletes who have made it to the level where they are competing in the career market or have competed in professional sports. The displayed behavior of the career professional or professional athlete although similar to the junior professional, is much more intense. These athletes or former athletes behave in a thoughtful, considerate manner and are self-assured of their current or previous role in sport. The assertive and ambitious approach taken towards sports, academics, and their career is how they now approach everyday life.

SELFLESS PROFESSIONAL ATHLETE EXAMPLE

As an example, a number of athletes have been successful in taking their sport-related experience and behavior to the political arena. According to businessinsider.com, examples of former athletes now successful in the political arena include: former NFL players Jon Runyan – U.S. Congressman (2010-present), Heath Shuler – U.S. Congressman (2007-present), Lynn Swann – Republican Candidate For Governor (2006), Steve Largent – U.S. Congressman (1994-2002), and Tom Osborne – U.S. Congressman (1995-2003). Players hailing from the NBA, Dave Bing – Mayor of Detroit, MI (2009-present), Kevin Johnson – Mayor of Sacramento, CA (2008-present) and Bill Bradley – U.S. Senator (1979-1997).[149]

Athletes that have been successful in the area of entrepreneurship during and after sport participation on the professional level according to fanchisehelp.com include: Earvin "Magic" Johnson, Max Montoya, Jamal Mashburn, Keyshawn Johnson, and Drew Brees to name a few. In looking at the mature behavioral approach taken by these athletes, their actions should serve as a blueprint for professional athletes regarding financial maturity.[150]

Earvin "Magic" Johnson

This Los Angeles Laker legend is now the gold standard for athletes turned entrepreneurs. The Magic Johnson Enterprise portfolio focuses on urban development and has included ownership interests in Starbucks (105 locations), TGI Friday's locations, Loew's Movie Theaters, a minority stake in the Lakers, and s a handful of other business interests. His travel franchise, Magic Johnson Travel Group, focuses on attracting multicultural franchisees that cater to the minority travel segment. The Magic Johnson Foundation supports HIV/AIDS and scholarships for inner city kids.

Max Montoya

This 16-year veteran played in four Pro Bowls and two Super Bowls with the Cincinnati Bengals. Montoya got started in franchising in 1995, and he now owns five Penn Station East Coast Subs restaurants in Kentucky. (Cincinnati-based Penn Station is a fast casual concept that serves hot and cold subs, hand-cut French fries, hand-squeezed lemonade and chocolate chunk cookies baked fresh in the restaurant.) Max's most recent Penn Station location opened in September, and he has plans to aggressively expand in the area. Not one to concentrate his wealth, Max is also an investor in several unrelated real estate properties.

Jamal Mashburn

This former NBA star, nicknamed "Monster Mash," was part of the "Triple J" Dallas Mavericks team, and along with Jason Kidd and Jim Jackson,led the franchise to the biggest turnaround in the NBA in 1994. Although he made over $75 million during his career, Mash decided not to rest on his laurels after his NBA career was over. Mashburn now owns 71 restaurants, including 34 Outback Steakhouse franchises and 37 Papa John's franchises. Mashburn also owns part of the Kentucky Derby horse Buffalo Man, along with Outback Steak House founder Chris T. Sullivan and his former coach at the University of Kentucky, Rick Pitino. (Side note: Pitino is himself a Dunkin' Donuts franchisee, which is weird, because Dunkin HQ is in Boston, and we all know that Ricky got himself run right out of Beantown).

Keyshawn Johnson

Just Give Me the Damn Ball! This Super Bowl Champion, best-selling author, and ESPN Analyst is also the CEO of First Picks Management, a business development company with an emphasis on franchises. Keyshawn's company recently opened several Panera Bread franchises throughout California. Keyshawn is not alone in these investments, as several NFL stars are investors in his firm, including Warrick Dunn, Dennis Northcutt, Reggie Bush and Terence Newman.

Drew Brees

This Super Bowl MVP got his first taste for Jimmy John's Gourmet Sandwiches at Purdue University. "I missed Jimmy John's so much from my time in the Midwest, and I thought that it was a great fit for what we were doing in New Orleans. The culinary arts is a big thing down here; there are great restaurants and great chefs; and so much of the culture is surrounded by food and dining. It's kind of neat to be a part of that somewhat by owning my Jimmy John's franchise," said Brees. Brees knows how to pick 'em: Jimmy John's Founder Jimmy John Liautaud has an impressive underdog story, going from finishing nearly dead last in his high school class to opening up one of the country's most popular sandwich chains. Liautaud was recently profiled on FranchiseHelp.com's roundup of the Ten Most Famous Franchise Founders of All Time (2011).

According to cnbc.com, the following is a list of other notable athletes that have been able to maximize the opportunity presented to them through their participation in professional sports.[151]

Oscar De La Hoya

Sports: By age 28, boxing's "Golden Boy" Oscar De La Hoya had won five titles in varying weight classes, making him the youngest boxer ever to win five world titles. He has a career total of ten championship belts and was a 1992 Olympic gold medal winner. He has generated $612 million in revenue for his 18 pay-per-view fights.

Business: De La Hoya is the top pay-per-view earner in ring history, bringing in more than $600 million. In 2000, he released Grammy-nominated music album "Oscar" in both English and Spanish. De La Hoya's management company, Golden Boy Promotions, consists of more than 40 fighters and numerous businesses, generating more than $100 million annually. De La Hoya personally owns more than fifty percent of the company.

Michael Jordan

Sports: Arguably the best basketball player known to the game, Michael Jordan changed the way basketball is viewed. He played for the Chicago Bulls and later for the Washington Wizards, totaling more than $90 million in earnings as a player salary.

Business: Currently, he owns the Charlotte Bobcats (which he bought for roughly $175 million) and is the face of Nike's Air Jordan sneakers. Other endorsements include: Gatorade, Wheaties, McDonald's, Coca-Cola, Chevrolet, Rayovac and Hanes. His estimated worth was more than $500 million before his divorce in 2006.

Venus Williams

Sports: Currently ranked Number Three in the world in singles and Number Two in doubles, Venus Williams is a professional tennis player who has redefined women's tennis. She pulled in $15.5 million from playing this year, according to Forbes.

Business: Williams is currently CEO of her interior design firm "V Starr Interiors." She also launched her own fashion line in 2007. She is part owner of the Miami Dolphins with her sister, Serena. In 2001, she signed a five-year endorsement contract with Reebok International for $40 million. Her new book "Come to Win" was Number Five on the New York Times Best Seller list. She was ranked number 83 on Forbes' 2010 Celebrity Top 100 list.

Tony Hawk

Sports: Sponsored by the age of 12 and pro at 14, Tony Hawk changed the face of the skateboarding world. Over the next 17 years, he entered more than 100 pro contests, winning 73 of them and placing second in 19. In 1999, Tony Hawk landed the first-ever "900" at the X games— two and a half spins mid air! In total, Hawk invented more than 80 tricks.

Business: Hawk is the owner of Birdhouse, one of the largest skateboarding companies in the world, and he started his own clothing line, aptly named "Hawk Clothing." He has deals with Activision, Six Flags, Kohl's, Infospace, Adio shoes, Jeep and Sirius Satellite Radio. In conjunction with Activision, Hawk created Tony Hawk's Pro Skater Video game in 1999, which quickly became a best seller, now making him the Number One action-sports video game franchise. Tony continues to release video games for all gaming systems. He also released an autobiography, which was a New York Times bestseller. Hawk grossed $12 million in 2008 alone, according to Forbes.

John Elway

Sports: Although originally drafted to the Baltimore Colts, John Elway played for the Denver Broncos. His initial contract with the Broncos was for a 6 year, $12.7 million contract. He is best known for his 15-play, 98-yard offensive series in the AFC Championship game, aptly known as "The Drive." He helped lead the Broncos to five Super Bowl appearances and two wins.

Business: Since retirement, he has owned several businesses and writes an NFL blog. He also founded The Elway Foundation, a non-profit organization for the prevention of child abuse. He is also the owner of two restaurants and once owned five car dealerships in the Denver area. He sold them to AutoNation in 1997 for $82.5 million. He is still in the car dealership business.

LeBron James

Sports: Drafted directly out of high school to the Cleveland Cavaliers, LeBron James is said to show talent on the same level as Michael Jordan. Earning $19 million in his first four years with the Cavs, James recently signed with the Miami Heat for a little less than $16 million.

Business: Before James even signed with the Cavs, Nike signed him to a seven year, $90 million contract. When Nike released his first shoe, Air Zoom Generation, it sold 72,000 pairs at $110 in its first month. He also owns his own marketing agency, known as LRMR, which secured endorsements with Nike, Sprite, Glacéau, Bubblicious, and Upper Deck. In 2010 alone, James totaled $30 million in endorsements.

George Foreman

Sports: This heavyweight champion took the boxing world by storm with his most notable fight "Rumble in the

Jungle" against Muhammad Ali for the world heavyweight title in Zaire, Africa. Although he lost the fight, he pulled in more than $5 million for the fight alone. He won the gold medal in the 1968 Olympic Games for the United States. He was undefeated in 40 straight fights.

Business: Over 100 million George Foreman Grills have been sold worldwide. Foreman sold the marketing rights to his grills in 1999 for $137 million—more than what he ever made in his career as a boxer. His other business ventures include a clothing line, and a cleaning product line.

Dave Bing

Sports: This seven-time all-star is named one of the NBA's 50 greatest players. Starting out with the Detroit Pistons, over nine seasons Bing negotiated his contract from $15,000 up to $450,000. Later, he played two seasons for the Washington Bullets and ended his basketball career as a Boston Celtic. He was the sixth rookie in NBA history to top 1,600 points and held a record of 18,372 points for his career total.

Business: In 1980, Bing launched Big Steel in Detroit. Within a decade, his steel mill was pulling in $61 million in annual sales, making Big Steel the 10th largest African American-owned industrial company in the nation. He later founded Superb Manufacturing, a $28 million-per-year metal stamping company. As chairman of Bing Group, an automotive supplier, he has sales of over $200 million.

Vinnie Johnson

Sports: Seen as one of the greatest "sixth men" in basketball history, Vinnie Johnson helped lead the Detroit Pistons to numerous NBA victories. He is best known for sinking the winning shot in the 1990 NBA finals against Portland with 00.7 seconds left in the game. That same year, he held out on resigning his contract until he signed for $3.2 million in a two-year agreement.

Business: After retirement, Johnson founded Piston Automotive. The company now has more than 200 employees and sales of over $85 million.

Cal Ripken Jr.

Sports: This Baltimore Orioles shortstop is best known for breaking Lou Gehrig's record of consecutive games played—totaling 2,632 games. He is one of eight players in history to achieve 400 home runs and 3,000 hits. In 1992, he signed a five-year, $30.5 million contract to continue playing for the Orioles.

Business: As chairman and CEO of Ripken Baseball, Inc., Ripken helped build a baseball complex in his hometown of Aberdeen, Maryland. He owns the Augusta Green Jackets (the Class A affiliate of the San Francisco Giants), and the Charlotte Stone Crabs (the class A affiliate of the Tampa Bay Rays). A best-selling author, Ripken also has been the spokesperson for Energizer, Holiday Inn, Rinnai and State Farm Insurance.

Chris Webber

Sports: As a member of the Golden State Warriors, Chris Webber became the first NBA rookie to score more than 1,000 points, 500 rebounds, 250 assists, 150 blocks and 75 steals. He is a five-time NBA All Star. Webber remains the only sixth player in history to average more than 20 points, nine rebounds, and four assists per game. When he signed his contract again with the Sacramento Kings in for $123 million in 2001, his contract made him the second highest paid player in NBA history.

Business: Webber is active in investment companies representing basketball and football players, real estate and film projects. He had endorsement deals with Coca-Cola, EA Sports, Sony Playstation, ESPN the Magazine, Fila, Nike, Pepsi, Carl's Jr., THQ Wireless and New Era. He currently owns a real estate development company, Maktub LLC, which primarily focuses on redevelopment efforts in Chicago. He also opened his own restaurant in Sacramento, Calif., aptly named Center Court with C-Webb. He is also a music producer and is featured on numerous hip hop tracks.

Wayne Gretzky

Sports: Considered one of the greatest hockey players ever, Wayne Gretzky holds or shares 61 NHL records—40 for the regular season, 15 for the Stanley Cup playoffs and six for the NHL all-star game. He was paid more than $40 million from 1989 to 1999.

Business: Gretzky bought the Hull Olympiques of the Quebec Major Junior Hockey League for $175,000 CA, and he sold it seven years later for $550,000 CA. In 1992, Gretzky partnered with Bruce McNall in an investment to buy a rare Honus Wagner T206 cigarette card for $500,000 US. It most recently sold for $2.8 million US. He also owns his own restaurant, aptly named Wayne Gretzky's Restaurant, as well as his own winery. Forbes estimates he earned $93.8 mil between 1990 and 1998.

The athlete that takes advantage of his opportunities to explore his future while he is still competing is an example of the behavior athletes in this stage display. As an example, during the 2014 offseason Baltimore Ravens safety Matt Elam worked in a unique environment. Elam, as a first-round pick in the 2013 draft, started 15 games in his first season, and he worked 20 hours a week at a shoe store in a Gainesville, Florida. According to foxsports.com:

> Since Elam was a kid, he has wanted to eventually open his own sports merchandise store and saw this as his way to get some first-hand experience. Elam worked as a part-time sales associate, clocking about 20 hours per week. He worked on the floor and occasionally stocked the shelves in the back. Elam also attended classes at the University of Florida to finish up his degree. Elm's reason for working in a shoe store was, "I just need to get retail knowledge," Elam said. "That's basically what I'm doing. I'm getting that knowledge for when it's time." Everybody was surprised when I started," he said. "They were like, 'Why? You got enough money.' But it's not about the money. It's just me building. "I know you can't do football forever. I'm going to use it to benefit me when I'm doing so that my kids won't have to worry about this," Elam said. "I take a lot of pride in that because I feel like a lot of kids are blind to this and don't have these opportunities, and don't have the knowledge. I hope I can open a lot of their eyes."[152]

These athletes are completely different from those in the other categories because they are now playing sports for money and they see opportunities in sports as business opportunities. This section is not implying that all professional athletes play only for money, but rather that for athletes at this level, playing sports is their job. These athletes, like those in *The Selfish Stage*, branch out into separate classes of athletes. Some of them agree to endorse or advertise any product in order to make more money; others only endorse or advertise the products they actually use, while others develop their individual brand as a business. Although there are many other ways athletes in this category differ, the salient point is that they do all differ.

Summary

The athlete, much like the monarch butterfly, experiences a long developmental journey. The variety of internal and external factors associated with the overall developmental process can determine if the athlete will develop into a healthy person after his/her athletic career is exhausted, or in the case of the caterpillar, transform into a beautiful butterfly. We witness athletes achieve success out of sports and after they have exhausted their playing careers. Until now, we have not been able to explain some of the defining factors associated with this behavior.

The behavior of the athlete has been a mystery to many, and the developmental stages make a significant breakthrough in understanding athlete behavior as well as labeling athlete behavior. Athletic departments and professional organizations must focus on the early behavioral warning stages of an athlete to ensure they have a healthy and productive experience in sport. Providing blanket statements after an athlete experiences a behavioral climactic episode, as previously discussed, is a cookie cutter reaction and a nonchalant approach to providing an athlete with the necessary services.

The *Starter*, *Selfish*, and *Selfless* behavioral stages affect the athletes' personal, social, and professional development in a variety of ways. The three areas of the selfish stage: criminal, academic, and financial, are the key behavioral areas that ultimately affect every aspect of the athlete journey inside and outside of the sporting environment. For example, getting arrested for a felony or suffering academic defeat can affect your ability to become gainfully employed. In the case of careless spending, poor financial decisions can have long-term implications on your family dynamics, personal relationships, and an athletes' mental health. These are just a few of the many examples athletes exhibiting negative behavior will encounter. On the other hand, the athlete who is free of criminal activity and excels academically has a better chance of adjusting to life outside of the sporting environment. The professional athlete who is financially savvy has the opportunity to establish healthy family, social, and business relationships. At the same time, they adjust to life outside of the sporting environment with the same drive and passion displayed while he or she is a competitive athlete.

Some could argue that it is not the responsibility of university athletic departments and professional organizations to be concerned with the behavioral developmental process of the athlete. My counter argument is simple, understanding the behavioral stages of the athlete under the personal player development umbrella will give coaches, athletic directors, and associated personnel a better chance to provide real personal development services for the athlete. This ultimately results in a better athlete and a better person, who at the end of the day, will end up being a more productive person and player.

Further, I would argue that providing athletes with the necessary development skills is in fact the *responsibility* of coaches, athletic directors, and associated personnel, as they are the ones knowingly placing the athlete on a pedestal. How can these individuals expect to create an invincible athlete, and then feign ignorance when time and again athletes are caught displaying negative behavior as a direct result of their feeling of invincibility? If we take this questioning one step further, we must also ask the extent to which racism is perpetuated by the current athletic system. As the majority of top performing athletes in signature sports are African American, and the media eagerly headlines any news related to yet another black athlete in trouble with the law, we must begin to seriously question the role that colleges, professional organizations, and coaches play in maintaining systemic racial oppression and stereotypes within our society. The need for personal player development has never been more salient.

CHAPTER SIX
PRACTICAL METHODS: STEPS MOVING FORWARD

Scoundrels use wicked methods, they make up evil schemes to destroy the poor with lies, even when the plea of the needy is just. [Isaiah 32:7]

VETTING AND FOLLOW-THROUGH SERVICES

Every college athletic department and professional organization should have a vetting and follow-through process for potential athletes. The vetting process needs to be led by, or should at a minimum include, an internal or external personal development helping professional. The process should consist of an investigation of relationships and behavior, as well as an entry interview and exit interview.

Most professional teams have a vetting process in place. However, many of these teams fail to develop a personal development strategy to address the questionable issues that have been raised through the vetting process. Most often, the professional teams are dealing with personal development issues that have been overlooked by college officials, which makes the task of assisting the young professional a challenging one. Another setback for professionals working with athletes from a personal development stand point is the format they use to assist the athlete over an extended period of time.

The collegiate level desperately needs to interject a vetting process. A vetting process on the collegiate stage would take care of two issues. One, it would allow coaches an opportunity to determine which athletes are in need or at risk in the areas of personal, social, and professional development and two, it would give helping professionals a starting point with all athletes to ensure they are receiving the necessary personal development. The vetting process is an opportunity to find everything an organization needs to know about an athlete they plan on investing time and money into.

WORLD WIDE WEB AND ATHLETIC IDENTITY

The letters WWW have become well known for World Wide Web. These three letters are fixtures in our daily lives, but for the athlete in the described athletic identity model, WWW means so much more, and it is a starting point to either developing or discovering their true identity as well as a point of focus for the athlete. Prior to working with athletes from any level of sports, I ask the Athletic Identity WWW (AI-WWW) questions as seen in figure 15. These questions are the essence of holistically exploring athletic identity. Without addressing these questions with an athlete, the helping relationship is considered artificial.

I find an athlete's answers to these simple yet also complicated questions useful in developing a plan to meet the athlete's overall personal developmental expectations. Most helping professionals spend countless hours engaging with athletes. They make all types of attempts to assist the athlete, but they never get to the point of clarifying the athlete's individual expectations. Prior to an athlete's first high school sporting competition or before signing an athletic scholarship or a professional contract, helping professionals and parents should consider asking these three questions under the athletic identity umbrella:

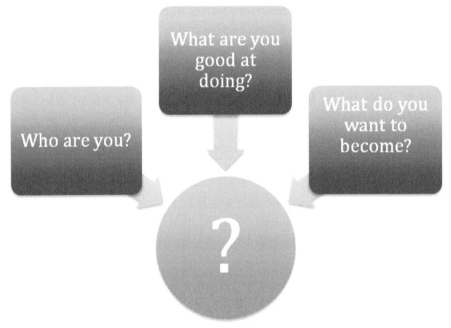

Figure 15. WWW, Questions

Ask any high school, college, or professional athlete these questions, specifically in the signature sports, and require an answer that excludes sport, and I am sure you will find many blank expressions on the faces of these athletes. The WWW questions under the athletic identity umbrella are the single most effective method of investigating where an athlete is headed in the athletic identity perspectives. The Initial, Invincible, Invisible, In-Between, or Independent athletic identity perspectives all can be quickly identified through an observation of the age of the athlete, and an athlete's answers to these three questions. As mentioned throughout the course of this book, the areas of personal, social, and professional development are the three overarching components that make up personal player development. In a practical sense, athletes must understand the developmental process early on. The following Q and A were taken from an interaction with a high school student seeking my assistance in his personal development.

> Dr. Mark: Who are you?
> John: I am John, and I am a high school football player.
> Dr. Mark: What are you good at doing?
> John: Scoring touchdowns.
> Dr. Mark: What do you want to become?
> John: A professional football player.

The first answer, although it identifies John, also tells us what he does, which is specifically how he is identifying himself. Some might argue playing football is not who you are, it is what you do, but I disagree. If playing football is all John has known since the age of five or six, it is easy to believe football is what John does as well as who John is. John is identifying himself through name and sport, and he believes his identity is based on football. The answers from John are common for athletes on all levels depending on the sport. As an athlete begins to explore personal development options, the answers should change if athletes are provided with an opportunity to explore real world developmental options.

The AI-WWW questions and answers set the tone for the work that lies ahead. Some athletes will require more work than others to develop answers that exclude sport. Others may be able to articulate their answers better due to the external contributors discussed previously. A method of application of the AI-WWW questions, and how they are interjected into athletes' personal development is discussed later in this chapter.

THE THREE HOLISTIC PERSONAL PLAYER DEVELOPMENT PROGRAM STRANDS

Athletic departments, athletes, parents, and coaches are primarily concerned with eligibility, graduation, game schedule, uniforms, number of games on TV, and playing time. The professional organizations are concerned with turning a profit and winning a championship. While these things all have value, no one seems to be truly concerned about the personal development format or program that will help develop and prepare the athlete for life during and after sports participation. Ask any college recruiter, academic specialist, or athlete development staff member to show you their four-year program for personal development, and I doubt that you will get information in the same manner you receive an answer regarding eligibility, game schedule, uniforms, tickets, jersey sales, and number of games on TV. A recruiter or coach typically tells a parent that they will make sure the athlete stays on track to graduate and will get everything needed to be successful in life after sport. However, I know from interacting with athletes on a daily basis from a variety of institutions that they are not receiving the needed personal development. Although initially indicated by recruiters and coaches, personal development is usually not a priority, winning is.

As discussed in chapter two, a holistic personal player development program should include a unique curriculum designed for the athlete, as outlined in table 5. The topic areas needed to provide athletes with a holistic approach towards personal development have been established through years of working with athletes on a global scale. The intended curriculum allows organizations, athletes, and helping professionals a starting and ending point. The program curriculum is divided into three development categories: the Personal, Social, and Professional development strands. Athletic identity and decision-making are the only topics that cover all categories across the developmental strand areas. The curriculum being presented is targeting the collegiate athlete, although a number of key elements should be included in the development of the professional athlete as well.

The curriculum strands do not have to be delivered in a particular order with the exception of athletic identity because, as mentioned earlier, athletic identity is the starting point to understanding who an athlete is, the work that they need to accomplish, and who they will become.

ATHLETIC IDENTITY

This is the starting point to helping athletes fully understand what it really means to be an athlete, and it is also the starting point to assisting them in exploring a positive balanced and healthy lifestyle. The topic of personal development is introduced, as well as the need for personal development for athletes, and the stages of athletic identity; all of which have been the focus of this book. Collectively, these topics lay the foundation for athletes, allowing them to develop a complete understanding of athletes and athlete behavior.

PPD Foundation

PERSONAL	SOCIAL	PROFESSIONAL

Curriculum Topics

Athletic Identity	Athletic Identity	Athletic Identity
Relationship Issues: Fatherhood, motherhood Family Ties	Cultural Competency	Career Exploration: Guidance from Start to finish
Health and Wellness: During and After Sport Participation	Casual Relationship Development	Image: Brand Development and Protection
Spirituality of the Athlete	The Justice System and Athletes	Network and Media Development
Finance	Fan Appreciation	Education: Academic and Professional Courses
Leadership and the Decision Making Process	Leadership and the Decision Making Process	Leadership and the Decision Making Process

Table 5. Curriculum Topics and Strands

PERSONAL DEVELOPMENT STRAND

The areas of Relationship Issues, Health and Wellness, Spirituality of the Athlete, and Finance cover the personal development strand of the athlete. This area of the curriculum is designed to give the athlete all the necessary basic fundamental development needed during the transition phase of an athlete's journey through sport. These four general topic areas have an abundance of sub-topics that can and should be explored. For example, the health and wellness topic has many interrelated dimensions of wellness: physical, emotional, intellectual, spiritual, social, environmental, and occupational. Each dimension is equally vital in the pursuit of optimal health.

SOCIAL DEVELOPMENT STRAND

The athlete will experience challenges associated with his or her social interactions, particularly face-to-face interaction. Cultural Competency, Casual Relationship Development, The Justice System and Athletes, and Fan Appreciation are the subject areas in the social pillar that will help athletes in the area of self-perception, and the external perception others have of them. Again, the general topics in the social development of the athlete are accompanied by a variety of sub-topics. As an example, Cultural Competency can explore diversity in various types of disabilities, sexualities, religious beliefs, race, and nationality.[153]

PROFESSIONAL DEVELOPMENT STRAND

Career Exploration, Image and Brand Development, Network and Media Development, and Academic and Professional courses are interjected to help athletes in their preparation for future careers in the workplace or professional sports. The four general topics in the professional section are intended to place importance on life during and more so after sport participation. This area is likely the most under-used area by colleges, particularly the athletic departments, because many do not see the benefit in aggressively assisting the athlete in this area. Sure, they may have career day, resume writing, and degree attainment, which is good. However, these activities all consist of paper and electronic documents to define the athlete, leaving athletes and institutions with a prehistoric method of gravitating towards becoming a career professional. For example, Image and Brand Development is a topic that in many ways works on behalf of the college and the individual athlete, and it consists of many sub-topics.

The American Marketing Association defines a brand as the "name, term, design, symbol, or any other feature that identifies one seller's goods or service as distinct from those of other sellers."[154] Your brand identity is the representation of your company's reputation through the conveyance of attributes, values, purpose, strengths, and passions.[155] The athlete is a by-product of the institutional athletic department's brand. Most athletes do not see the relationship between themselves and the respected institution in this manner. According to Forbes magazine, whether you are on the job hunt, a student, or gainfully employed, you must think, act, and plan like a business leader. With the surge of social media, you have not only the ability, but you now have the need to manage your own reputation, both online and in real life.[156] For athletes, this has never been truer, yet few athletes share this proactive mindset.

The professional development strand focuses on preparing athletes to build their own professional brand.

LEADERSHIP & DECISION MAKING

This is a major area of the PPD curriculum and is just as important as the area of athletic identity. Athletes are anointed leaders by virtue of sports participation, and the decisions they make affect everyone around them as well as themselves. Once a young person dedicates his or her time towards sports, they have incorporated themselves in the business of sports. They in fact must become CEO's of themselves. Making key life decisions along the sport-filled journey can build or ruin the company, which in this case is the athlete. As the CEO of YOU Inc., athletes need to understand the key areas of decision-making from a corporate standpoint, and they must apply them to their daily routine. Although we tend to focus on leadership in the sporting environment, the area of Leadership and Decision Making in the PPD curriculum is directly connected to the decision making process outside of the sporting environment. Some of our athletes find themselves on the wrong side of the law. This is due to the poor decisions they made.

THE PPD FOUR-YEAR COLLEGE CURRICULUM PROGRAM

The introduced PPD curriculum can be delivered and broken down in a multitude of ways depending on the time one has with athletes. Courses and seminars are a great way to deliver the curriculum. Some topics can be delivered over the course of a semester and others in a few hours. The key ingredient is to have every topic covered in detail over the tenure of the athlete. As seen in table 6, the topics are carefully grouped, allowing freshman, sophomore, junior, and senior athletes the opportunity to explore the personal, social, and professional areas of development each year while they also experience the journey through sports. In total, the curriculum provides six topics per year for athletes. While that may seem like significant content, if we look at the amount of time athletes are on campus, particularly the "down time" athletes have during the holiday and summer time, there is more than enough time to cover six topics in a year.

FRESHMAN YEAR

As mentioned, the topic of Athletic Identity is one that must be covered across a four year period starting with the freshman student athlete, simply because the topic of athletic identity and related stages is one athletes will encounter over the course of their college career and possibly, if fortunate, their professional career. The number of athletes we are witnessing making poor decisions highlights the need for the topic of Leadership and Decision Making to be offered across a four-year period as well. Other PPD topics for the freshman athlete should include Casual Relationship Development, Health & Wellness During and After Sport Participation, and Education: Academic and Professional.

The exploration of careers and professional opportunities is key because most freshman college students, including athletes, are unsure about their major and career goals. Covering these topics during a student athlete's freshman year will allow athletes and helping professionals an opportunity to start a holistic journey for the athlete's personal development.

PPD Curriculum Four-Year College Program

FRESHMAN	SOPHOMORE	JUNIOR	SENIOR
Year by year Curriculum Topics			
Athletic Identity	Athletic Identity	Athletic Identity	Athletic Identity
Casual Relationship Development	Fan Appreciation	Cultural Competency	The Justice System and Athletes
Health & Wellness: During and After Sport Participation	Spirituality of the Athlete	Finance	Relationship Issues: Fatherhood/Motherhood Family Ties
Career Exploration: Guidance from Start to Finish	Network and Media Development	Image: Brand Development and Protection	Further Education Exploration: Academic and Professional Courses
Leadership and the Decision Making Process	Leadership and the Decision Making Process	Leadership and the Decision Making Process	Leadership and the Decision Making Process

Table 6. PPD Four-Year Curriculum

SOPHOMORE YEAR

By the time a student athlete reaches their sophomore year, they are in a more comfortable place regarding the student athlete journey. These athletes have managed to get through their first year of college academically, and in most cases, are excited to experience a new role on an athletic team. We expect student athletes to be better athletes each year in their sport, and the expectations for the sophomore student athlete are higher than for freshmen. However, we cannot expect the athlete to personally develop without program offerings. During a student athlete's sophomore year, the PPD topics one should consider covering are Fan Appreciation, Spirituality of the Athlete, Networking and Media Development, as well as Athletic Identity and Leadership and Decision Making as previously mentioned.

JUNIOR YEAR

Having survived the first two years of college, athletics is an accomplishment and should be treated as such. However, the work in the area of personal development for the junior student athlete is where a dramatic peak should occur. The athlete has experienced the athletic identity perspectives thus far, highlighting the importance of an athlete's final two years of college. The topics of focus for the junior student athlete are Cultural Competency, Finance, Image and Brand Development as well as Athletic Identity and Leadership and Decision Making. The junior student athlete needs to now focus on the life they desire once sport participation is complete, regardless of their chances of playing professional sports. Personal development for the athlete is a preparation for what is guaranteed to come—the real world. It also prepares athletes for something they all will experience—retirement.

SENIOR YEAR

The senior student athlete and helping professionals should understand that preparation for exiting athletic identity began their freshman year, and in a little more than 365 days an athlete's identity will undoubtedly change. We are witnessing thousands of athletes each year that have a difficult time adjusting to life after sports participation. Most institutions and helping professionals focus on life after college, after college is over. This puts the athlete in a horrible situation as it pertains to recovering a new identity. A student athlete entering their senior year will have few questions regarding personal development if they have been introduced to the topics in the PPD curriculum. The following topics should be covered during a student athlete's senior year: the Justice System and the Athlete, the Former Athlete, Relationship Issues, Further Education Exploration, as well as Athletic Identity and Leadership and Decision Making. These topics target the exiting athletic identity phase of a student athlete's sports journey and emphasize a reentry to the real world phase. This reentry into the real world process is one that many athletes abandon between the ages of six and ten.   If athletes are privileged to receive a holistic personal development approach, this will allow the athlete to invest time and emotions into figuring out who they are now that their athletic journey has come to an end.

THE ROLE OF A PPD COLLEGIATE HELPING PROFESSIONAL

Now that a curriculum has been presented, focusing on the role of the PPD professional is a key connecting point to ensuring the curriculum is delivered effectively. A person working with athletes and doing it the right way will understand each athlete on campus represents a job lasting 1,460 days *per* athlete. Yes, a holistic program for student athletes includes the mentioned curriculum but is driven by the full-time assistance of a PPD helping professional. A large part of the PPD curriculum can and should be taught by either an individual, or a team of individuals, working as part of the athletic department's student athlete/wellness development or life skills unit.

A helping professional assisting athletes in the area of personal development must understand the position is not a nine to five one. Instead it is closely linked to an emergency room doctor; you never know when you are going to be needed so you are on call, as well as providing daily assistance for the athletes under your care. Teaching, counseling, group work, and listening are all major components of the position. The goal of the helping professional is to develop athletes from the *Initial* athletic identity perspective and to see them through to the *Independent* athletic identity perspective with the understanding of the need to assist athletes in bypassing the *Invincible*, *Invisible*, and *In-Between* perspectives.

The role of the PPD helping professional is not a life coach The last thing an athlete needs is another coach assisting them that is called "coach." The role is defined as a Personal Development *Specialist*, *Consultant*, or *Director*. The process of assisting athletes from one stage of development to the next is a facilitation of personal growth. A year-by-year example of the role of the helping relationship is as follows:

FRESHMAN YEAR

We have already established the topic of athletic identity as a must for all freshmen. Ideally, this course should be taught by the helping professional hired to work in the student athlete/wellness development or life skills unit. This gives the athlete and helping professional a great start towards building a solid four-year relationship with each other.

The WWW questions, which are a big factor in the athletic identity course, are to be asked and explored during individual meetings. In most cases, these three questions will lead to one-on-one meetings with athletes. Individual meetings with athletes during their freshman year should be mandatory, but since they are currently not required, it is the helping professional's job to earn the respect of the athlete, which will result in the athlete wanting to meet. If not, establishing a working relationship with coaches is the best direction, which may be difficult, but is not impossible. During a student athlete's freshman year, it is important to create an academic educational plan. However, it is also critical to create a personal development plan.

All meetings must have objectives or a helping professional will have a difficult time tracking growth, goals, and will find meeting an athlete's needs challenging. Each meeting must review the objectives from the previous meeting. If the previous meeting objectives were not met, it is pointless to move forward on newly stated objectives as the unfinished business needs attending to. Individual meetings do not necessarily have to take place on campus, and in some cases meetings are more free-flowing off campus away from the athletic facility. The following are examples of exercises and objectives of individual meetings with athletes you might find useful in building a relationship:

- Videotaped memoir of athlete's experience in sport prior to college
- WWW, essay
- Create an expectation chart including external contributors
- Create an individual expectation chart on athletics, academics, and career
- One-on-one meeting review

SOPHOMORE YEAR

By the time a student athlete enters their sophomore year, helping professionals and athletes should have developed a solid relationship. This relationship will be built on a combination of the personal development course, and the one-on-one meetings during the athlete's freshman year. The helping professional should have a good idea regarding the type of athletes he or she is working with, as well as what their individual needs are. This is a great time to introduce athletes to the area of group meetings. Group meetings with athletes should be based on their stage of athletic identity. These group meetings should not take the place of individual meetings unless the athlete and helping professional feel the individual meetings are no longer necessary. However, this is rarely the case, as athletes will continue to seek assistance if the relationship has been beneficial and personal growth has occurred. Some of the other methods suggested when working with sophomore student athletes includes:

- Videotaped memoir of athlete's experience in sport and what they have done to develop their personal developmental plan (5min)
- WWW essay freshman review and redraft
- Review the expectations of external contributors (recorded)
- Review of individual expectation and data on athletics, academics, and career pursuits
- Group and (one-on-one if necessary) meetings

JUNIOR YEAR

At this point, student athletes are half way through their 1,460 days and helping professionals have only 730 days left to assist the athlete in his/her overall development. The junior student athlete year is a major preparation year for their graduation year. Athletes and helping professionals should approach their junior year as if it is in fact their senior year. This approach eliminates athletes from waiting until the last minute to see what life is like in the real world. More importantly, it gives the athlete and helping professional a chance to see what needs to be accomplished in order to have a stress-free transition from one phase of sport participation to the next, in this case leaving college. The following examples of exercises could be applied to junior athletes:

- Videotaped memoir of athletes experience in sport and what they have done to develop their personal developmental plan (5min)
- WWW essay sophomore review and final draft
- Review expectations of external contributors (recorded)
- Review of individual expectation and data on athletics, academics, and career pursuits.
- Transitional groups and (one-on-one if necessary) meetings

SENIOR YEAR

This is the last year of an athlete's journey in collegiate athletics and should be the most exciting. This time should be exhilarating in the sense that the athlete has been afforded the luxury to develop a solid plan for the future with or without sport participation. Transitioning from sports will have emotional and physical effects on the athlete. However, if the athlete has been involved in a holistic developmental program as the one described, the emotional and physical effects of the transition will be minimized and student athletes will encounter a considerable amount of joy moving forward.

The senior student athlete will require individual meetings very similar to the meetings that took place during an athlete's freshman year. The student athlete as a senior, regardless of the preparation for their exit from college, will need help in the creation and development of a list of new expectations moving forward. The original WWW questions will be a foundation and method that athletes will use in their personal, social, and professional development after their collegiate career, and will change over time. The examples of exercises and activities for the senior student athlete include:

> Final videotaped memoir of athlete's experience in sport and what they have done to develop their personal developmental plan and advice to underclassmen (5min)
> WWW statement junior review and final
> WWW future statement
> Final review of expectations of external contributors recorded determine if expectations were met
> Final review of individual expectation data on athletics, academics and career pursuits to determine if expectations were met.
> Transitional and exit preparation groups and activities
> Final one-on-one exit interview with athlete and planning the follow through

THE PPD ROLE AND RATIONALE FOR ACTIVITIES

The activities suggested can be done in class, one-on-one with the athlete, or in small groups. The goal for athletes and helping professionals is to build a body of work that specifically reviews and explores the athlete's personal, social, and professional development over the tenure of their collegiate experience.

Videotaped memoir of athlete's experience in sport prior to college

This activity is designed to allow the athlete to express him or herself and to tell their story about the road they traveled to achieve the goal of playing college sports. This activity is not and should not be limited to sports, but it should discuss any challenges, family dynamics, and all of the relevant details about the athlete's personal background. The PPD professional has to be able to ask questions of the student athlete that will bring out the much-needed components of an athlete's personal story. Designing questions to get athletes to express themselves is not as difficult as it may seem if you are confident in why you are asking the specific questions. I encourage helping professionals to develop a set of questions that all athletes can answer.

WWW Statement

The student athlete's original WWW answers in most cases will be very similar to John's example provided earlier in this section. This is an important assignment which will be developed over the duration of the athlete's tenure at the institution. The goal is to progress John's original answers into a 15 to 30 second elevator pitch, eliminating (as much as possible) sports engagement. The charge for the PPD professional is to assist in the design and creation of answers from the student athlete's perspective. This activity can be written or videotaped. As an example, by the time John reaches his senior year of college, his answers should look like this:

> Who are you?
> *I am John Thomas, a son, brother, graduating senior majoring in marketing and a collegiate athlete*
> What are you good at doing?
> *Marketing and planning social events and assisting non-profits within the community*
> What do you want to become?
> *Eventually a marketing expert in the area of social media, but immediately land a position in one of the top social media firms in their marketing department.*

CREATE AN EXPECTATION CHART INCLUDING EXTERNAL CONTRIBUTORS

The expectation chart of the entitlement contributors is an activity where student athletes ask and record what these contributors are expecting from the athlete as a result of the college athlete experience. These expectations need to be electronically recorded and reviewed continuously. If a student athlete has a clear understanding of entitlement contributor's expectations of them, it can open the door to building respectful relationships with the individuals that may have access to opportunities after the athlete's sporting career is exhausted.

CREATE AN INDIVIDUAL EXPECTATION CHART ON ATHLETICS, ACADEMICS, AND CAREER

This is a great way to compare the athlete's expectations to the external contributors expectations, as well as determining early on what expectations are realistic. This method has been proven to eliminate stress and allow student athletes to develop the confidence needed to communicate freely to their entitlement contributors. When athletes engage with entitlement contributors regarding athletic identity, new interests, and new self-worth discoveries, the athlete begins to shape the future expectations of entitlement contributors. This establishes a new identity for the entitlement contributors to associate with the athlete.

Exploration of an athlete's expectations is vital to ensure that athletes maintain a healthy mental state. All freshmen athletes want to play, and as they move into their sophomore and junior year, the need to play becomes greater. If an athlete is not playing the amount of time he or she expects, the result can lead to academic defeat, poor effort in sport, transferring, criminal activity, and other negative behavior. The PPD role in this activity is to facilitate the process of the student athlete to continuously maintain an accurate focus on the original purpose of attending college: to receive an education. Without the assistance in exploring and establishing expectations, athletes will be less likely to thrive and more likely to struggle to survive during and after sport participation.

ONE-ON-ONE MEETING REVIEW

Without question, meeting one-on-one with student athletes is the most effective method in the PPD approach. This generation of athletes, as it pertains to communication, do not express themselves verbally in the same fashion as previous generations of athletes. This lack of verbal expression is due to the social media craze, so when and if athletes have the opportunity to engage in a face-to-face meeting, which is meant to allow them to express themselves, they love it. Some athletes can sit and talk face-to-face for hours, specifically if the conversation is designed to help them progress successfully. The role of the PPD professional in the one-on-one setting is again to facilitate a discussion in the personal, social and professional developmental areas. It should be noted that athletes will have issues and concerns about the coaching staff and playing time, and I would advise caution in giving advice in areas that the student athlete has little to no control over unless a crime or NCAA infraction has been committed.

GROUP MEETING

The second most effective method in the PPD approach is group meetings. This is an opportunity for helping professionals to create and facilitate an authentic diverse population of athletes from a variety of sports. Having student athletes meet from different backgrounds including gender, sexuality, religion, and socioeconomic status is a great way to build sport-specific relationships with other athletes in the department. In athletic departments today, the services and activities are segregated by sport. If they do include multiple sports, the athletes from particular teams tend to stick together. Strategic group meetings can cure this problem. Group meetings allow athletes the chance to engage with athletes that they, for the most part, do not know. Group meetings also allow athletes the opportunity to listen to other athletes' issues, concerns, future plans, etc.

PPD LEADERSHIP AND STAFF MEMBERS

Universities and professional teams have to become more transparent in their hiring practices when it pertains to the individuals charged with assisting in the growth and development of our athletes. We can no longer expect the coach, specifically coaches hired under the title of personal player development or student athlete development, academic advisors, or other staff members in athletics to take on the jack-of-all-trades role as it pertains to the personal development of athletes. There has been a new trend in hiring personnel for duties that do not align with the job title with football being the biggest culprit.

According to Jean Boyd, the Senior Associate Athletic Director for the Office of Student-Athlete Development at Arizona State University (ASU):

I think most of the institutions have someone who is dedicated to player development but you see it a lot more in football. Now, is that position mainly helping with recruiting, watching film, and in some cases coaching rather than actually focusing on personal player development issues? That could be the case. Having someone dedicated to work in the area of PPD would be good; it would allow athletes to engage on a different level. The folks in academics are probably the people dealing with athletes regularly, but many of these folks are busy working with athletes on the academic issues, not so much the personal development of athletes.[157]

As an example, the University of the Illinois Division of Intercollegiate Athletics, posted a job announcement entitled, Director of Football Student-Athlete Development. This position was announced as a twelve month, one-hundred percent academic professional appointment. The primary position function/summary was outlined as follows:

Manage all on-campus activities of student-athletes in the football program. Major responsibilities include: Manage all on-campus activities including but not limited to: Manage and coordinate all on campus admissions for incoming freshman and transfers, facilitate and develop campus relationships, liaison with Associate Athletic Director of Academics for football staff.

These duties, as well as others outlined in the job description, in no way address student athlete development in the context of personal development. Rather they address general understanding of the college and rules that govern athletics as they relate to the athlete. The position also identifies managing recruitment visits, ticket allocation, and preliminary transcript evaluations of high school and transfer prospects. This position is a coaching position and should be advertised as such.

Academic support services seem to be under pressure to provide personal development to student athletes. However, in their quest to meet this growing need they often push job announcements out without truly understanding the type of person needed to assist the athlete in personal development? As an example, the University of Missouri claimed to be seeking qualified candidates to fill four graduate assistantship positions in the Department of Intercollegiate Athletics. Two of the positions were slated to work in all facets of student athlete academic support services. The other two positions were slated to work under the Associate Athletic Director for Student Athlete Development, and again, assist in all facets of the student athlete.

The academic support service position responsibilities included: mentoring student athletes, monitoring student athlete academic progress, assisting with coordinating/supervising study halls as a learning supervisor, assisting with on-campus recruiting, assisting with hiring and scheduling of academic tutors, and preparing academic reports/assessments. The student athlete development responsibilities included: developing and implementing personal development programming, collaborating with community organizations to fill all community service requests, oversee the Tigers Cup Competition, serve as a staff liaison to the campus Student Athlete Advisory committee, coordinate all honors, awards, and scholarships, and assist in the career development center.

The requirements for these positions included a bachelor's degree in an appropriate discipline, a background in athletics, intent to work in the field of student athletic support services, excellent written and oral communication skills, a strong self-starter, excellent organizational skills, and great attention to detail. Although mentoring of athletes is a responsibility, it is not listed as a requirement, and one of the biggest problems with the student athlete development responsibilities in this job announcement is the assumption that a graduate assistant will be in the position to implement personal development programming. The above position announcement language is commonly used throughout athletics at the collegiate level and is not addressing the need for the personal development of athletes.

We rarely see job announcements for personal development positions on the professional level. This can be a combination of the limited number of positions, internal political network hiring, or promotions and overall company preference. On the professional level, hiring former athletes with no formal training or applicable degree in a related field should cease. Former professional athletes are best suited to work with current professional athletes because they have experienced the lifestyle. However, this is not always the case. When professional teams hire a former professional athlete to lead the personal development of athletes, often it is purely based on athletic experience. Rather, the required skills include a combination of education or degree attainment, practical experience working with athletes, training, and then athletic experience.

JOB REQUIREMENTS WHEN WORKING WITH ATHLETES

Degree: Holding a bachelor's degree does not afford degree holders the necessary academic understanding of what is needed to deliver personal development for athletes unless a significant, preferably yearlong, practical experience is included. Even then, the degree holder needs extensive experience working with athletes in the personal development arena as well as in the field of athletics as a participant.

Advanced degrees in fields such as Education, Psychology, Counseling, Sociology and the like are acceptable. A master's degree in the respected fields should directly focus on the area of personal development of athletes. For example, someone studying counseling who has a research focus on marriage and family is not considered qualified to work with athletes unless the focus of their study had a concentration on marriage and family within the athletic population. The same holds true for students at the doctoral level.

Experience: Experience as a former athlete is an absolute must for PPD professionals. How can you truly assist athletes if you have never been an athlete? This is not to say that a person with limited athletic experience cannot help in the area of personal development. However, the small daily issues that athletes face may hinder the helping professional if they have not experienced the pressures and challenges athletes face. Athletes are reluctant to seek help, and if a helping professional appears to be out of touch or unaware of the special circumstances specific to the athletic population, athletes will resist engagement in the helping process.

Training and Professional Development: Although the industry is in its infancy stages compared to other fields, would-be helping professionals need to seek out experts in areas identified in the PPD curriculum, as discussed previously. I would also encourage helping professionals to engage in research to establish roadways to best practices in these areas with the athlete as the control group as well as the intended audience. A major problem I have noticed over the years is the lack of professional development training afforded to helping professionals who are charged with working with athletes in the specific area of personal development. Conferences usually do not have extensive training for people who are working with athletes in a personal development capacity. Rather they are saturated with presentations, networking, sales booths, coffee, and socials.

SUMMARY

In athletics we use the term holistic in a way that makes me doubt we clearly know the true meaning of the word. Holistic is characterized by comprehension of the parts of something as intimately interconnected and explicable only by reference to the whole.[158] Building a holistic personal player development program requires a specific set of topics in three developmental areas: Personal, Social, and Professional. These three strands, regardless of the sub-topics introduced, must serve as the umbrella for a holistic program if institutions and professional teams want to develop athletes correctly.

The blueprint for a holistic program should be designed and delivered for athletes experiencing similar stages of academic growth. For example, the freshman personal development activities should not include sophomores and so forth. The intensity of the curriculum for freshmen and other classes must also be of a different magnitude. The most important component of a comprehensive program revolves around participation which is clear after years of interviews, discussions, and working with former and current athletes. The term holistic, although used often at the collegiate level, is not inclusive of all student athletes on campus, and in most cases program participation in development programs is not mandatory. Voluntary programs result in very low participation by athletes, which explains the problems athletes face during and after sport participation. The statement, "we can't make it mandatory" is a direct indication that the person making the statement does not have a great working relationship with the coach, because if they did, the coach would ensure mandatory participation.

In addition to mandatory athlete involvement, the success of development programs relies on the strength of the support staff. The helping professional working with athletes must establish a mutual level of respect. I often find helping professionals on college campuses who work with athletes in an attempted role of "friend." This relationship is not a healthy one for the student athlete simply because the personal developmental growth process requires strict discipline as well as a number of hard truths regarding the growth and level of maturity of the student athlete.

The current student athlete helping professional is in most cases using the job as a stepping stone or establishing a foot in the door of the collegiate athletic industry. The salaries for these positions rarely attract high quality experienced practitioners in the area of personal development. Academic support staff is often charged with the task of providing limited personal development services and are under pressure to meet the personal development demands of student athletes. In some cases, the athletic support staff have no choice but to simply sit back and watch the student athletes enter and exit the institution without the necessary skills needed to establish a new identity.

Arguably the biggest challenge facing current and future personal development staff members is gaining the necessary training in the area of personal development. Tony Robbins assists millions of people in the area of personal development and is considered one of the leading experts in the field. However, his research and implementation excludes the athletic population, leaving the athletic community without an advocate for training athletic helping professionals. The athlete needs specific personal development programs now more than ever, yet the number of academic degree programs targeting personal development of the athletic population is virtually nonexistent.

The structure of development programs is also essential. Small group and one-on-one sessions are integral to the personal growth of the athlete. Although athletes compete together, the area of personal growth for athletes requires individual attention. Getting to the heart of the AI-WWW will require a time commitment by both parties, and having a busy personal development program or activities during the off season will eliminate a large amount of stress and depression for the athlete once their season begins. Additionally, a large number of student athletes find themselves on the wrong side of the law during the off-season. Therefore, programs must fit into a busy schedule with the summer serving as the appropriate down time to focus on the personal development of student athletes.[159]

The leadership overseeing college athletics needs to understand the overall value and return on investment (ROI) for the athlete in the area of personal development. Leadership is out of touch regarding the needs of student athletes from a personal development stand point. Many of these leaders attended college and started their careers at a time when the stress and pressure of being a student athlete was not as prevalent as today. Although certainly not an excuse, this experience explains their lack of knowledge in the area being discussed.

As we move into the future, the professional and collegiate departments and organizations must make changes and additions to the services already in place. This should include how athletes are vetted, curriculum is designed, programs are structured, employees are hired, and future employees trained. Without this necessary change, the systemic patterns of selfish behavior, including negative criminal, academic, and financial activity will persist indefinitely. A successful personal development program for athletes, as outlined in this chapter, promises a complete transformation in the lives of athletes. A true holistic development program will promote athletes not only to be the best athlete they can be, but to make life their sport.

CHAPTER SEVEN
ATHLETIC CULTURE AND LEADERSHIP ON CAMPUS

Do not withhold good from those to whom it is due, when it is in your power to act [Proverbs 3:27]

SUMMARY

On June 27th, 2014, Indiana University (IU) Vice President and Director of Athletics Fred Glass introduced the Indiana University Student Athlete Bill of Rights. The document is a ten-point commitment to student athletes during their time as student athletes at IU and beyond. The document is being hailed as the first of its kind and intends to cover all phases of the student athlete's well-being and development. It comprehensively addresses subjects as wide ranging as post-eligibility degree support; scholarship commitment; academic, athletic, leadership and life skills development; career assistance; safety and medical care; meals and nutritional guidance; ensuring a culture of trust and respect; and collective student-athlete involvement within the athletics department.[160] The bill of rights includes a lifetime degree guarantee for student athletes, which is a major game changer in college athletics. According to Glass:

> We are proud to be the first higher education institution ever to publish a Student-Athlete Bill of Rights...We developed the Bill of Rights to identify not only what we were currently doing for our student-athletes but what we should be doing. We have committed to this extensive set of benefits and set it out transparently in writing, so that we can be held accountable for them by our student-athletes and other stakeholders such as our faculty and trustees. While no other school has done this, we hope that others will follow for the betterment of the student-athlete experience.

The specific component of the document that relates to the personal development of the athlete and the relevancy to this book is centered on the Leadership and Life Skills Development component. This includes the Indiana University Excellence Academy Speaker Series, the Indiana University Excellence Academy Internship Program, specialized social media training, and other programming. In addition, the Indiana University Excellence Academy Career Counseling and Placement Center helps to prepare student athletes to transition to the next phase of their lives, including successfully pursuing post college employment. The Center can also be utilized by former student athletes as may be needed during their careers after graduation.[161]

Many will speculate that the IU student athlete bill of rights serves the place of payment that athletes should receive for their efforts, and they would be right. IU can make a good argument that this commitment to the student athlete comes at a cost, and there is a dollar amount that can be placed on each athlete. Throughout countless decades, student athletes have been dedicated to IU or their respective institutions, only to have their efforts and personal development needs go unnoticed. Although the experience differs for individual athletes, many seem to feel forgotten as former players.

The IU athletic leadership has taken a bold step with their Student Athlete Bill of Rights document, and others across the country in all divisions should take note and follow suit on the idea and implementation of such a commitment to the student athlete. How knowledgeable IU decision makers are on the topic of athletic identity, and the needed curriculum to create a holistic personal development program is yet to be seen. However, the overall intent and document is a start. I hope the area of personal development for athletes becomes more than a "check-the-box" notion for the future of the IU athletic department and does not become watered-down with a focus on clinical implementation as opposed to personal development, as I believe college athletics will be looking to their leadership in this area.

LEADING THE TRIBE ON CAMPUS

If the case for the need to embrace athletic identity on all levels of sports has not been made yet, or you are one of the people that do not believe athletes are a unique population who demand personal development specifically for their issues, then let's take a look at the student athlete experience and the non-student athlete experience by reviewing the culture on our academic campuses.

The Native Americans, or American Indians, consisted of many tribes such as the Cherokee, Mohawk, Oneida, Onondaga, Cayuga, Seneca, and Tuscarora. We know from history that tribes were located in specific parts of the USA. Each tribe established their rituals, style of dress, and creation of art and customs, which made them all unique as well as valuable in laying the foundation for the USA. The key to a successful tribe was the understanding and development of tribal members, which required effective leadership. In most cases, the tribes communicated with other tribes, but rarely integrated.

Today our college campuses in many ways mirror the organizational structure of ancient tribes. Faculty unions, administration, academic departments, student clubs and organizations, and athletics each have their own unique systems. The two most exclusive student-related tribes on campus are 1) athletics and 2) the Greek system. The Greek system includes all-inclusive organizations where members often sleep, dine, study, engage in community service activities, and also bring in speakers to talk exclusively to their membership. Like ancient tribes, the key to developing student athletes requires an understanding of the student athletes' needs, as well as effective leadership.

THE ATHLETIC DEPARTMENT IS A TRIBE

If we view the athletic department as one of many tribes on campus, athletics could be regarded as one of the leading tribes due to the amount of attention, energy, athletic performance-based resources, and facilities dedicated to athletics. Athletics also has customs, styles of dress (many uniforms and colored shoes), mascots, and rituals. The leadership in athletics (athletic directors AD, associate AD's, coaches), and it's members (athletes and employees), are responsible for increasing the effectiveness and development of the tribe and its members. Why send student athletes to integrate with non-student athletes when athletics is the leading tribe and has all of the necessary tools, mainly funding, to holistically personally develop their own members [athletes]? When examining the student athlete compared to the non-student athlete overall, we find the foundation needed for career attainment is in the daily rituals of the student athlete. However in many cases the student athlete takes on one of the stages of athletic identity and will too often forego the career development opportunity afforded with the student athlete experience.

STUDENT ATHLETES, ATHLETIC IDENTITY, AND NON STUDENT ATHLETE EXPERIENCE

In an article written by Daniel Keys, he explains that to be adored by fans and compete on national television is a once in a lifetime opportunity. The endorphins released from such adulation are part of an experience that non-student athletes and fans do not often experience. For athletes, sports are a place of refuge. The athletic arena provides comfort, and it is a place of escape for whatever an individual may have been through, currently dealing with, or dreaming of. However, it is finite, and it is a predetermined means to an end. Most people in the sports industry, on any level, understand this fact. However, most athletes just do not understand that their time in sport is limited.[162]

Keys continues, "Who wouldn't want glory, adulation, and the perks associated with being great to last forever?"[163] That's exactly what athletes experience and desire. This starts at an early age. In many instances, this experience is a monocular view and a single-sided approach and experience. This one-sided approach, in many cases, leads to the athlete abusing the entitlement label often given in sports today. The high school athlete entering college will either enjoy the short-term athlete experience or enjoy the long-term benefits of being a student athlete. The difference between the two is simply their approach to the decisions and choices made during a four or five year process.[164]

ATHLETIC IDENTITY

We often hear athletes say that the sports field or court is where they are most comfortable. Understanding how to work with students who take on the full-time identity of an athlete is an area very few are skilled in, nor fully understand, including the athletes themselves. Concentrating on this area is an absolute necessity because most athletes see themselves as just an athlete. According to Chris Spielman during an interview on College Football Live which aired on ESPN in 2012:

> I made mistakes because I defined myself purely as a football player, and I'm a little bit embarrassed. In a newspaper, I made this statement: 'I wanna play football; I wanna coach, and I wanna die.' That's pretty shallow; fortunately I was humbled enough and I transitioned from a shallow man into a complete man. I was humble enough to learn lessons, relied on other people and let go of my arrogance.[165]

Arrogance is demonstrated both by the athlete as well as those that make up or encompass the parts of the athletic system. High schools have an assembly for athletes making a decision on what school they will be attending to play sports. However, the same school could have several future Ivy League students in the audience. These students do not have an assembly announcing their acceptance of a merit-based academic scholarship to schools of choice for their academic and scholarly pursuits.

As a result of these young men and women engaging in such an act of egoism and narcissism, they step on campus with lofty expectations. Fans, media, coaches, family, and so forth help the athlete create an identity that is strictly engulfed in sport, which is why so many athletes step on campus and utter the words, "I'm here to play football, basketball, etc."[166] Thus, there is no focus on personal, social, or professional career development.

Athletes become so consumed with solely taking on the identity of being just an athlete that they do not know who they are when the uniform comes off. Realistically, an individual's sport should be complimentary of who they are and prepare athletes for adulthood. That way, when it's time to close a particular chapter in an individual's life, there may be sadness, but there is also peace. To lead to such a positive outcome, the question "who are you?" must be asked the first day an athlete steps on campus.

For the student athlete, practice and games are structured and require attendance. Academic preparation including tutors and study time require attendance as well. In many cases, there are consequences for missing class; appointments with helping professionals are required, and finally, the athlete's social life and any non-sport related activities are all under the microscope of social media which means no hiding. Athletes rarely miss practice, injured or otherwise, and work hard to maintain eligibility status. The student athlete experience also includes a social element like no other, and this social element is accompanied by the larger campus community tribes. The student athlete is the main part of the student experience and in many cases the signature of the college. When we think of Duke, we think of the Blue Devils, IU, the Hoosiers and Cal, the Bears. Often, these major institutions are most recognized for their signature athletic programs.

NON-STUDENT ATHLETE EXPERIENCE

With respect to the student experience, being a non-student athlete includes possibly working one or two jobs, networking, enjoying certain campus and community based activities, as well as a concentration on studying, which athletes undertake in one form or another. The student experience also has another side. This may include tailgating, fraternity parties, lazy weekends, and missing class without immediate consequences from coaching staff members. Non student athletes have the ability to call into work sick and hang out with friends without having their academic or athletic status jeopardized unlike the student athlete. The non-student athlete experience, in most cases, is heavily weighed in the activities and success surrounding the athletic program of their respected institutions. Therefore, when I hear athletic administration continuously call for the student athlete to encounter the non-student athlete experience, I often wonder if athletic leadership understands what the non-student athlete experience really is all about. Leadership in athletics has to become proactive in the personal development of the athlete and move away from trying to integrate the student athlete with non-student athletes when it specifically comes to the personal development of the athlete. This is simply because the collegiate experience for the student athlete and non-student athlete are totally different.

Leadership In Athletics

Anyone in the athletic department has the ability to lead. Someone in the athletic department must begin to advocate and embrace the personal player development movement. According to Godin in his book, Tribes: We Need You to Lead Us, great leaders create movements by empowering the tribes to communicate. Athletic personnel need to start communicating the need for personal developmental services and activities specifically targeting the student athlete population and graduate from the status quo of integrating student athletes with non-student athletes regarding personal development. Integrating student athletes with non-student athletes for personal development purposes is not conducive to the overall personal development of the student athlete; it is a matter of status quo. Organizations that destroy the status quo win. Individuals who push their organizations, who inspire other individuals to change the rules, thrive.[167]

The athletic department is a highly visible tribe in higher education, and the student athlete is a member of this tribe establishing them as a campus and community leader. These leaders require personal development services and activities tailoring their experience. As mentioned, groups on campus such as fraternities and sororities function as all-inclusive, providing their membership the necessary tools to develop by providing tailored-made services. Therefore, why do we place such high emphasis on the student athlete integrating when it pertains to personal developmental activities? It is time for athletic leaders and advocates to embrace holistic programs and services for the personal development of the athletes, and more importantly, to make the resources available to have the right people in place.

Finally, I hope this text serves as the first of many books dedicated to the holistic implementation of curriculum, activities, methods of application and more importantly, understanding athletic identity in the area of personal development for the athlete. More research and practical methods of application are needed as the stakes in athletics become even higher, or our athletes will become engulfed in their athletic identity.

[1] www.beyondsuccess.com
[2] Wikipedia, 2012
[3] Mary Ellen Leicht, 2013
[4] Interview with Jim Carr by Dr. Mark Robinson for www.ppdmag.com. January 28, 2014.
[5] Interview with Jim Carr by Dr. Mark Robinson for www.ppdmag.com. January 28, 2014.
[6] Interview with Lamonte Winston by Dr. Mark Robinson, 2013
[7] Interview with Lamonte Winston by Dr. Mark Robinson, 2013
[8] Interview with Kim Durand by Dr. Mark Robinson for www.ppdmag.com. February 10, 2013.
[9] http://dictionary.reference.com/browse/personal?s=t
[10] Wikipedia, 2013
[11] Interview with Mary Ellen Leicht by Dr. Mark Robinson for www.ppdmag.com. July 14, 2013.
[12] Interview with Dr. William Broussard by Dr. Mark Robinson for www.ppdmag.com. July 10, 2013.
[13] Interview with Kevin Greene by Dr. Mark Robinson for www.ppdmag.com. April 13, 2013.
[14] Interview with Greg Taylor by Dr. Mark Robinson for www.ppdmag.com. August 28, 2013.
[15] Interview with Marviel Underwood by Dr. Mark Robinson for www.ppdmag.com. August 28, 2013.
[16] Interview with Jocelyn Gebhardt by Dr. Mark Robinson for www.ppdmag.com. August 28, 2013.
[17] Interview with Kristy Belden by Dr. Mark Robinson for www.ppdmag.com. May 16, 2013.
[18] Interview with Dr. Howard Bartee by Dr. Mark Robinson for www.ppdmag.com. July 10, 2013.
[19] Interview with Gary Darnell by Dr. Mark Robinson for www.ppdmag.com. July 10, 2013.
[20] Tom Ferraro (http://www.athleticinsight.com/Vol6Iss2/IsPDF.pdf) 2004
[21] Interview with Chris Thomas by Dr. Mark Robinson for www.ppdmag.com. May 16, 2013.
[22] http://bleacherreport.com/articles/1656181-how-much-responsibility-does-a-college-coach-have-for-a-players-academics. 2013
[23] http://bleacherreport.com/articles/1656181-how-much-responsibility-does-a-college-coach-have-for-a-players-academics. 2013
[24] Interview with Jeff Janssen by Dr. Mark Robinson for www.ppdmag.com. November 2, 2013.
[25] Interview with Jamil Northcutt by Dr. Mark Robinson for www.ppdmag.com. May 16, 2013.
[26] Interview with Jeff Janssen by Dr. Mark Robinson for www.ppdmag.com. November 2, 2013.

27 Interview with Dan Dakich by Dr. Mark Robinson for www.ppdmag.com.
February 4, 2013.

28 Interview with Lamonte Winston by Dr. Mark Robinson, 2013

29 Dr. Harry Edwards Biography. https://www.nflplayerengagement.com/news-and-media/black-history-month/articles/bhm-feature-dr-harry-edwards/.
2013.

30 nflplayerengagement.com, 2013

31 Poll conducted by Dr. Mark Robinson for www.ppdmag.com. Kirk Dixo posted
his response. 2013.

32 Petitpas and Brewer, 1996.

33 http://growingleaders.com/blog/abandonment-or-abundance/

34 http://sportsillustrated.cnn.com/nfl/news/20130619/aaron-hernandez-history/

35 Interview with Kelly Jordan Diener by Dr. Mark Robinson for
www.ppdmag.com. April 14, 2013.

36 Interview with Chris Herren by Dr. Mark Robinson for www.ppdmag.com.
April 12, 2013.

37 Brewer, W.B., Van Raalte, J.L., & Linder, D.E. (1993). Athletic identity: Hercules'
muscle or Achilles' heel? International Journal of Sport Psychology, 24, 237-254.

38 psychologyabout.com

39 Originally posted on www.ppdmag.com on June 13, 2013 for the article
LinkedIn: Student-Athlete to Career Professional, A Trail of Transitional
Reflections.

40 Dave Crowder, www.ppdmag.com, 2013.

41 Wikipedia, 2013: http://en.wikipedia.org/wiki/World_view

42 Interview with Megan Pulido by Dr. Mark Robinson for www.ppdmag.com.
January 11, 2014.

43 Interview with Scooter Barry by Dr. Mark Robinson for www.ppdmag.com.
February 8, 2013.

44 Interview with Kristin Lundy by Dr. Mark Robinson for www.ppdmag.com.
June 12, 2013.

45 Interview with Jennifer Abercrumbie by Dr. Mark Robinson for
www.ppdmag.com. June 6, 2013.

46 Minnesota Amateur Sports Commission. Minnesota Amateur Sports
Commission, Athletic Footwear Association, USA Today Survey, Michigan State,
2013 http://www.statisticbrain.com/youth-sports-statistics/

47 Youth Sports Statistics ,
http://www.facupwardsoccer.com/youthsportsstatistics.htm

48 Results originally published in: ppdmag.com, 2013

49 Interview with Gary Darnell by Dr. Mark Robinson for www.ppdmag.com. July
10, 2013.

50 SBnation.com, 2013: The wildest National Signing Day stories, from Willie
Williams to Davonte Neal, http://www.sbnation.com/college-football-

recruiting/2012/2/22/2816287/college-football-recruiting-davonte-neal (February 3 2014)

[51] http://www.cnn.com/2014/01/07/us/ncaa-athletes-reading-scores/
[52] Interview with Jim Livengood by Dr. Mark Robinson, 2012
[53] http://www.cnn.com/2014/01/07/us/ncaa-athletes-reading-scores/
[54] http://www.cnn.com/2014/01/07/us/ncaa-athletes-reading-scores/
[55] http://www.cnn.com/2014/01/07/us/ncaa-athletes-reading-scores/
[56] http://www.cnn.com/2014/01/07/us/ncaa-athletes-reading-scores/
[57] Harper, S. R., Williams, C. D., & Blackman, H. W. (2013). Black male student-athletes and racial inequities in NCAA Division I college sports. Philadelphia: University of Pennsylvania, Center for the Study of Race and Equity in Education.
[58] Interview with Albert Jennings by Dr. Mark Robinson for www.ppdmag.com. March 13, 2013.
[59] Interview with Jessi Greenberg by Dr. Mark Robinson for www.ppdmag.com. March 13, 2013.
[60] Interview with Kelly Jordan Diener by Dr. Mark Robinson for www.ppdmag.com. April 14, 2013.
[61] Interview with Kevin DeShazo. ppdmag.com, 2014.
[62] Sports Illustrated http://sportsillustrated.cnn.com/basketball/news/2002/09/09/webber_indicted_ap/ Posted: Monday September 09, 2002 3:14 PM; Updated: Tuesday September 10, 2002 10:12 PM
[63] Sports Illustrated http://sportsillustrated.cnn.com/basketball/news/2002/09/09/webber_indicted_ap/ Posted: Monday September 09, 2002 3:14 PM; Updated: Tuesday September 10, 2002 10:12 PM
[64] Interview with Akbar Gbaja-Biamila by Dr. Mark Robinson for www.ppdmag.com. February 13, 2013.
[65] Interview with Lawrence Funderburke by Dr. Mark Robinson for www.ppdmag.com. February 2, 2013.
[66] Sports Illustrated http://sportsillustrated.cnn.com/nba/news/20140131/anthony-bennett-cleveland-cavaliers-chris-grant/
[67] Interview with Mary Ellen Leicht by Dr. Mark Robinson for www.ppdmag.com. July 14, 2013.
[68] Interview with Kelly Jordan Diener by Dr. Mark Robinson for www.ppdmag.com. April 14, 2013.
[69] Interview with Cynthia Barboza by Dr. Mark Robinson for www.ppdmag.com. April 12, 2013.
[70] Interview with Cynthia Barboza by Dr. Mark Robinson for www.ppdmag.com. April 12, 2013.
[71] Interview with Cynthia Barboza by Dr. Mark Robinson for www.ppdmag.com. April 12, 2013.

[72] Interview with Cory Dobbs, www.ppdmag.com, 2014.

[73] Interview with Sheri Acho, www.ppdmag.com, 2014.

[74] Interview with Athena Liao by Dr. Mark Robinson for www.ppdmag.com. March 13, 2013.

[75] www.ppdmag.com, 2014.

[76] Matt McCarthy, Odd Man Out: A Year on the Mound with a minor league Misfit (London, England, Penguin Group, 2009), pp. 287-9.

[77] Interview with Scooter Barry by Dr. Mark Robinson for www.ppdmag.com. February 8, 2013.

[78] Interview with Marviel Underwood by Dr. Mark Robinson for www.ppdmag.com. August 28, 2013.

[79] Interview with Akbar Gbaja-Biamila by Dr. Mark Robinson for www.ppdmag.com. February 13, 2013.

[80] Interview with Cynthia Barboza by Dr. Mark Robinson for www.ppdmag.com. April 12, 2013.

[81] Interview with Marviel Underwood by Dr. Mark Robinson for www.ppdmag.com. August 28, 2013.

[82] Interview with Cynthia Barboza by Dr. Mark Robinson for www.ppdmag.com. April 12, 2013.

[83] The MAP dual-theory was developed as a result of the findings from the author's doctoral dissertation research (1998) and practical application in consultation with athletes (1998-Present).

[84] Interview with Athena Liao by Dr. Mark Robinson for www.ppdmag.com. March 13, 2013.

[85] Mark Robinson, 1998: Black Athletes Perceptions on Counseling Service in American Universities

[86] Mark Robinson, 1998: Black Athletes Perceptions on Counseling Service in American Universities

[87] Eddie George: I fought 'demons' after NFL, http://www.tennessean.com/article/20140205/SPORTS01/302050095/Eddie-George-fought-demons-after-NFL February 5th 2014

[88] Mark Robinson, 1998: Black Athletes Perceptions on Counseling Service in American Universities

[89] Eddie George: I fought 'demons' after NFL, http://www.tennessean.com/article/20140205/SPORTS01/302050095/Eddie-George-fought-demons-after-NFL February 5th 2014

[90] Eddie George: I fought 'demons' after NFL, http://www.tennessean.com/article/20140205/SPORTS01/302050095/Eddie-George-fought-demons-after-NFL February 5th 2014

[91] Memoir of an Athlete, by Donnie Tasser. Originally posted on www.ppdmag.com. May 16th, 2013. Donnie Tasser is a former wrestler and two times NCAA Qualifier at the University of Pittsburgh. He graduated with honors in 2013 with degrees in History and English Writing and has aspirations of

becoming a sports journalist. Reach him by email at donnie.tasser@gmail.com or on twitter at @DonnieTasser

[92] Interview with DeQawn Mobley. Published on ppdmag.com. February 5th, 2013.

[93] Eddie George: I fought 'demons' after NFL, http://www.tennessean.com/article/20140205/SPORTS01/302050095/Eddie-George-fought-demons-after-NFL February 5th 2014

[94] Eddie George: I fought 'demons' after NFL, http://www.tennessean.com/article/20140205/SPORTS01/302050095/Eddie-George-fought-demons-after-NFL February 5th 2014

[95] Mark Robinson, 1998: Black Athletes Perceptions on Counseling Service in American Universities

[96] Memoir of an Athlete, by Jay Keys. Originally posted on www.ppdmag.com. May 17th, 2013.

[97] Interview with Jessie Greenberg by Dr. Mark Robinson for www.ppdmag.com. March 13, 2013.

[98] Interview with Jessie Greenberg by Dr. Mark Robinson for www.ppdmag.com. March 13, 2013.

[99] Interview with Albert Jennings by Dr. Mark Robinson for www.ppdmag.com. March 13, 2013.

[100] Interview with Albert Jennings by Dr. Mark Robinson for www.ppdmag.com. March 13, 2013.

[101] Interview with Albert Jennings by Dr. Mark Robinson for www.ppdmag.com. March 13, 2013.

[102] Interview with Akbar Gbaja-Biamila by Dr. Mark Robinson for www.ppdmag.com. February 13, 2013.

[103] Johnny Manziel Thrown Out Of Frat Party At University Of Texas, http://www.huffingtonpost.com/2013/07/29/johnny-manziel-frat-party-university-texas_n_3670668.html. Posted: 07/29/2013. 01.18.13

[104] In an interview with Jon Gruden, Johnny Manziel admits mistakes both on and off the field. http://www.dallasnews.com/sports/college-sports/texas-aggies/20140327-in-interview-with-jon-gruden-johnny-manziel-admits-mistakes-both-on-the-field-and-off.ece. March 27th, 2014.

[105] The Definitive Timeline Of Lance Armstrong's Apparently Doped-Up Career, http://www.buzzfeed.com/nicholasschwartz/a-definitive-timeline-of-lance-armstrongs-career, January 15, 2013.

[106] Oprah Winfrey's Best Lance Armstrong Interview Moments, http://www.thedailybeast.com/articles/2013/01/18/oprah-winfrey-s-best-lance-armstrong-interview-moments-video.html

[107] Tiger Woods affair story, http://www.betus.com.pa/sports-betting/golf/articles/tiger-woods-affair-story/.

[108] Kobe Bryant charged with sexual assault, http://www.cnn.com/2003/LAW/07/18/kobe.bryant/. December 16, 2003

[109] Kobe Bryant charged with sexual assault,
http://www.cnn.com/2003/LAW/07/18/kobe.bryant/. December 16, 2003
[110] The MAP dual-theory was developed as a result of the findings from the author's doctoral dissertation research (1998) and practical application in consultation with athletes (1998-Present).
[111] Butterfly Questions and Answers: how many butterflies species are there http://www.naba.org/qanda.html
[112] Mark Robinson, 1998: Black Athletes Perceptions on Counseling Service in American Universities
[113] Na'im Akbar, Visions for Black Men (Mind Productions, Tallahassee, Florida) 1991
[114] Cass Tech QB Jayru Campbell, set to play Michigan State football, arrested after video surfaces
Jan 22, 2014, http://www.wxyz.com/news/video-cass-tech-football-player-body-slams-security-guard
[115] Cass Tech QB Jayru Campbell, set to play Michigan State football, arrested after video surfaces
Jan 22, 2014, http://www.wxyz.com/news/video-cass-tech-football-player-body-slams-security-guard
[116] 3 Somerville High School Soccer Players Arrested On Rape Charges
http://boston.cbslocal.com/2013/08/30/3-somerville-high-school-jv-soccer-players-arrested-on-rape-charges/ (August, 2013)
[117] ASU's Sean Price suspended after arrest
http://www2.wataugademocrat.com/News/story/UPDATE-ASUs-Sean-Price-suspended-after-arrest-id-012330 (2013)
[118] ASU's Sean Price suspended after arrest
http://www2.wataugademocrat.com/News/story/UPDATE-ASUs-Sean-Price-suspended-after-arrest-id-012330 (2013)
[119] ASU's Sean Price suspended after arrest
http://www2.wataugademocrat.com/News/story/UPDATE-ASUs-Sean-Price-suspended-after-arrest-id-012330 (2013)
[120] Ex-ASU football player charged with assault:
http://www.journalnow.com/news/local/article_aa1885d0-3540-11e3-b2e2-001a4bcf6878.html (2013)
[121] ASU football player charged with assault,
http://www2.wataugademocrat.com/News/story/ASU-football-player-charged-with-assault-id-013466. (2013)
[122] ASU football player charged with assault,
http://www2.wataugademocrat.com/News/story/ASU-football-player-charged-with-assault-id-013466. (2013)
[123] ASU's Blair charged after traffic stop,
http://www2.wataugademocrat.com/News/story/ASUs-Blair-charged-after-traffic-stop-id-012568.

[124] http://www2.wataugademocrat.com/News/story/ASU-football-player-charged-with-assault-id-013466

[125] ASU linebacker charged with assault, http://www2.wataugademocrat.com/News/story/ASU-linebacker-charged-with-assault-id-008575. (August 2012)

[126] ASU linebacker charged with assault, http://www2.wataugademocrat.com/News/story/ASU-linebacker-charged-with-assault-id-008575. (August 2012)

[127] ASU athletes won't face rape charges: http://www2.wataugademocrat.com/News/story/ASU-athletes-wont-face-rape-charges-id-007856.

[128] ASU Basketball Player Arrested: http://www2.wataugademocrat.com/Sports/story/ASU-basketball-player-arrested-id-003912

[129] Redskins TE Fred Davis arrested for DUI on day after NFL suspends him indefinitely http://www.washingtonpost.com/sports/redskins/redskins-te-fred-davis-arrested-for-dui-on-day-after-nfl-suspends-him-indefinitely/2014/02/20/506ab9c0-9aaa-11e3-b88d-f36c07223d88_story.html

[130] Henderson arrested for DWI; Simpson pleads guilty to DWI-related charges, http://www.startribune.com/sports/vikings/238466101.html (2014).
Suns release Michael Beasley, citing 'personal and professional conduct standards:" http://nba.si.com/2013/08/06/michael-beasley-arrested-marijuana-possession-phoenix-suns/. September 03, 2013

[131] Sources: Michael Beasley to Suns, http://espn.go.com/nba/story/_/id/8131044/sources-michael-beasley-verbally-commits-three-year-18-million-deal-phoenix-suns. 2012

[132] Suns release Michael Beasley, citing 'personal and professional conduct standards:" http://nba.si.com/2013/08/06/michael-beasley-arrested-marijuana-possession-phoenix-suns/. September 03, 2013

[133] Sources: Michael Beasley to Suns, http://espn.go.com/nba/story/_/id/8131044/sources-michael-beasley-verbally-commits-three-year-18-million-deal-phoenix-suns. 2012

[134] Suns release Michael Beasley, citing 'personal and professional conduct standards:" http://nba.si.com/2013/08/06/michael-beasley-arrested-marijuana-possession-phoenix-suns/. September 03, 2013

[135] Suns release Michael Beasley, citing 'personal and professional conduct standards:" http://nba.si.com/2013/08/06/michael-beasley-arrested-marijuana-possession-phoenix-suns/. September 03, 2013

[136] Pensinger, 2013
Suns release Michael Beasley, citing 'personal and professional conduct standards:" http://nba.si.com/2013/08/06/michael-beasley-arrested-marijuana-possession-phoenix-suns/. September 03, 2013

[137] Heat sign Michael Beasley to non-guaranteed, minimum contract, http://nba.si.com/2013/09/11/michael-beasley-miami-heat-contract-sign-agreement-phoenix-suns/. 2013

[138] Na'im Akbar, Visions for Black Men (Mind Productions, Tallahassee, Florida) 1991

[139] USC Guard Greg Allen Declared Academically Ineligible, http://www.conquestchronicles.com/2013/1/4/3836006/usc-guard-greg-allen-declared-academically-ineligible January 4, 2013

[140] FSU's Haulstead Declared Academically Ineligible, http://miami.cbslocal.com/2013/08/09/fsus-haulstead-declared-academically-ineligible/ (August, 2013)

[141] Texas Longhorns declare three players academically ineligible for Alamo Bowl, http://fansided.com/2013/12/22/texas-longhorns-declare-three-players-academically-ineligible-alamo-bowl/. December, 2013

[142] Demetrius Walker and Jeff Lowery dismissed from Grand Canyon team, http://collegebasketballtalk.nbcsports.com/2013/12/27/demetrius-walker-and-jeff-lowery-dismissed-from-grand-canyon-team/ (December 2012)

[143] Demetrius Walker and Jeff Lowery dismissed from Grand Canyon team, http://collegebasketballtalk.nbcsports.com/2013/12/27/demetrius-walker-and-jeff-lowery-dismissed-from-grand-canyon-team/ (December 2012)

[144] Demetrius Walker and Jeff Lowery dismissed from Grand Canyon team, http://collegebasketballtalk.nbcsports.com/2013/12/27/demetrius-walker-and-jeff-lowery-dismissed-from-grand-canyon-team/ (December 2012)

[145] Demetrius Walker and Jeff Lowery dismissed from Grand Canyon team, http://collegebasketballtalk.nbcsports.com/2013/12/27/demetrius-walker-and-jeff-lowery-dismissed-from-grand-canyon-team/ (December 2012)
GCU Men's Hoops Add Demetrius Walker to 2013-14 Roster, http://www.gculopes.com/news/2013/7/10/MBB_0710130511.aspx, 2013.
http://www.azcentral.com/sports/asu/articles/2010/04/20/20100420ex-arizona-state-sun-devils-guard-demetrius-walker-to-new-mexico.html, 2010
http://collegebasketballtalk.nbcsports.com/2013/07/10/grand-canyon-adds-former-new-mexico-guard-demetrius-walker/, 2013.

[146] Broke, http://espn.go.com/30for30/film?page=broke (2012)

[147] http://www.celebritynetworth.com/articles/celebrity/broke-athletes/

[148] Professional Athletes Who Have Gone Broke, http://www.celebritynetworth.com/articles/celebrity/broke-athletes/ October 3, 2012

[149] 12 Pro Athletes Who Became Successful Politicians, http://www.businessinsider.com/12-professional-athletes-turned-politicians-2011-5#kevin-johnson--mayor-of-sacramento-ca-2008-present-3. (2011)

[150] The All-Franchising Team: Top Pro Athletes Who Own Franchises: https://www.franchisehelp.com/blog/top-professional-athletes-who-own-franchises/. (2011)

[151] 15 Pro Athletes Turned Entrepreneurs, http://www.cnbc.com/id/38359640/page/1.

[152] NFL player's awesome reason for working at shoe store during offseason, http://msn.foxsports.com/buzzer/story/matt-elam-baltimore-ravens-working-in-a-shoe-store-during-offseason-022614. (February, 2014)

[153] Craig E Author, Cultural Diversity: Discussion Topics, http://cearthur.files.wordpress.com/2012/06/cultural-diversity-discussion-topics.pdf, 2013

[154] American Marketing Association: https://www.ama.org/resources/Pages/Dictionary.aspx?dLetter=B&dLetter=B

[155] Steve Hall, The Marketer's Guide to Developing a Strong Brand Identity http://blog.hubspot.com/blog/tabid/6307/bid/34238/The-Marketer-s-Guide-to-Developing-a-Strong-Brand-Identity.aspx, 2013

[156] The First Step To Building Your Personal Brand: http://www.forbes.com/sites/dailymuse/2012/02/14/the-first-step-to-building-your-personal-brand/, 2012

[157] Interview with Jean Boyd. Available at: http://ppdmag.com/jean-boyd-of-asu-the-athletic-and-academic-landscape/. March 13th, 2013.

[158] Apple dictionary

[159] arrestnation.com

[160] IU Announces Unprecedented Student-Athlete Bill of Rights. June 27th, 2014. http://www.iuhoosiers.com/genrel/062714aab.html

[161] http://www.iuhoosiers.com/genrel/062714aab.html

[162] Daniel Keys, 2013. http://ppdmag.com/the-student-athlete-experience-vs-the-athletic-experience/

[163] Daniel Keys, 2013. http://ppdmag.com/the-student-athlete-experience-vs-the-athletic-experience/

[164] Daniel Keys, 2013. http://ppdmag.com/the-student-athlete-experience-vs-the-athletic-experience/

[165] Chris Spielman, 2012. ppdmag.com/the-student-athlete-experience-vs-the-athletic-experience/

[166] Daniel Keys, 2013. ppdmag.com/the-student-athlete-experience-vs-the-athletic-experience/

[167] Seth Godin, Tribes: We Need You to Lead Us (London, England: Penguin Group) 2008

CPSIA information can be obtained
at www.ICGtesting.com
Printed in the USA
FSOW03n1613271115
13670FS